Letts Guides to Sugarcraft

Side Designs

ADRIAN WESTROPE

CHARLES LETTS · *Letts* of London® · FOUNDED 1796

Dedication

I would like to dedicate this book to the memory of a very special friend, Eddie, who died suddenly last summer, and to his wife, Trish, and their children.

First published 1992
by Charles Letts & Co Ltd
Letts of London House
Parkgate Road
London SW11 4NQ

Designed and edited by
Anness Publishing Ltd
1/7 Boundary Row
London SE1 8HP

ISBN 1-85238-316-X

A CIP catalogue record for this book is available from the British Library.

Editorial Director: JOANNA LORENZ
Designer: PETER BRIDGEWATER
Photographer: SUE ATKINSON
Illustrator: LORRAINE HARRISON

Printed and bound in Italy

Contents

Foreword

Adrian and I have been friends since our schooldays, and we later worked for the same high class bakery and patisserie. It was here that I was first struck by Adrian's original approach to his work and his interest in side designs, in particular. This book illustrates many different decorating styles that can be applied to cake sides, including a host of exciting and innovative ideas developed by Adrian himself, such as the paste-weaving technique applied to cutter inlays, and his interpretation of fabric designs and metalwork techniques to create novel side designs.

With this excellent book for guidance you will never again be lost for ideas when deciding how to decorate cake sides, for the following cake projects, although complete in themselves, also offer endless ways of adapting the designs with different colour schemes and for different occasions. I am sure you will enjoy many hours looking through this book and will be inspired to follow the side designs and experiment with your own ideas.

NICHOLAS LODGE

Introduction

When giving a demonstration to a group some years ago, I can remember one person saying to me afterwards, 'Side decoration often presents a problem, as you are rather limited as to the amount of actual piping that can be carried out on the side of a cake in comparison to what can be achieved on the top'. For this person and many others, I hope that the side designs described here will change your minds.

Quite often the side decoration on a cake is neglected, which is such a pity as there is a wealth of space and scope on which to work. In most cases decorators spend time making items for the top of the cake, such as flowers and ornaments, but forget to decorate the sides significantly. This book is designed to give ideas, instructions and objectives for the sides of cakes. It does not matter if you are a novice cake decorator or more experienced. My aim is that you will use the information and pictures that follow, and that your skills will improve. In time, using your own imagination, you will be able to create ever more attractive and elaborate side designs to complete your cakes.

The methods which follow are put together to allow you to create your own designs, as well as copying those in front of you. Some of the ideas incorporate several different techniques, showing how they can be combined to give a variety of colour, texture and depth to the cake sides. Many of the designs in this book are created for 20 cm (8″) square cakes and, with the exception of a few, can be adapted to fit practically any shape. All the patterns can be altered to suit larger or smaller cake sides.

I find that there are many different ways to obtain ideas in the form of patterns for cakes. To progress from the designs I have shown to forming patterns of your own, use that which is around you. For example, carpets, rugs, ceramics, mosaics, architectural details, paintings and pavement patterns. Ceramic designs – birds, butterflies and flowers in strong vibrant colours – also work well on cakes.

Not all the ideas are conventional. I have tried to mix and match my patterns to create some unusual and original side designs. Different approaches to texture, style and colour should be taken into consideration when you begin to extend the ideas I have given. For I hope you will find the cake sides I have designed an inspiration for further development, thereby helping me to achieve my aim to promote the skills of cake decoration and design in others.

ADRIAN WESTROPE

Equipment

Most of the equipment listed here and used in the book is relatively inexpensive and easy to obtain. Make use of standard household items whenever possible and buy specialized equipment only when really necessary. For example, a sharp kitchen knife and ruler will serve in place of the mint cutter or pizza wheel when cutting thin equal strips of Mexican paste for off-set ribbons or quills. Thin dowels rods can be used as formers for curving paste; but remember to line such items with Quick Release Sheet or grease with vegetable fat so the paste can be removed easily.

It is always much easier to work on side designs if the cake is tilted. For this reason, a cake tilter is invaluable and it can be used with a turntable.

1 pencil
2 cardboard for templates
3 ready-cut templates
4 glass-headed dressmakers' pins
5 Quick Release Sheet (QRS)
6 button embossers
7 ivy leaf cutter
8 small sharp scissors
9 continuous anglaise cutter
10 clay gun and forming discs
11 selection of piping tubes
12 smoother
13 cake tilter
14 turntable
15 hexagonal cakeboard
16 icing (confectioners') sugar dredger (shaker)
17 greaseproof paper (baking parchment)
18 cornflour (cornstarch) sieve

19 stainless steel rolling pin
20 mini whisk
21 spring hair grips
22 cocktail sticks (toothpicks)
23 confectioners' varnish
24 edible paste and powder colours
25 colour palette
26 mini plunger cutters in heart and blossom shapes
27 anglaise eyelet cutter
28 selection of plain round and oval cutters
29 crucible
30 sugar glue
31 mint cutter
32 foam
33 selection of pastry brushes
34 selection of paintbrushes
35 pizza wheel
36 & 37 tweezers

38 craft knife
39 sharp long-bladed kitchen knife
40 palette knife (spatula)
41 melon baller (parisienne cutter)
42 butter curler
43 crimper
44 clean-up tool
45 scriber
46 selection of modelling tools
47 ribbed rolling pin
48 parchment piping bags (cones)
49 non-stick rolling board
50 white glitter dusting powder
51 rolled fondant (sugarpaste)
52 appliqué flower (bleeding heart)
53 Mexican paste pine cones
54 quills
55 tiny plunger cutter flowers

Note

Piping tubes come in a wide range of sizes. Most of the piped work described in this book has been completed using writing (plain) tubes in the following sizes: No. 00 (the finest nozzle), 0, 1, 2, 3 and 4. Other tubes used are No. 5, 42, 43 and 44; they are toothed and are used to make textured shell and scroll designs.

Basic Techniques

TEMPLATES

All the cakes featured in this book describe a particular sugarcraft technique – appliqué, overlay, panelling, crimping, criqué and embroidery work, to name just a few – and some combine several techniques. However, in most cases you will need to know how to make an accurate template before beginning any decorating work on the cake sides. Templates are used in two basic ways: as a greaseproof paper (baking parchment) pattern guide for scribing a design on to the cake surface; and as a cardboard shape to cut around.

Transferring a Design to Card

In many cases a template can be made by simply tracing the master design on to greaseproof paper (baking parchment). However, if a more substantial template is needed, transfer the design to cardboard. The following instructions apply to all straight-sided cakes (see page 10 for curved cakes).

- Cut the greaseproof paper and cardboard to fit the cake side. Trace the chosen design on to the greaseproof paper with a pencil.
- Turn the greaseproof paper face-down on to the card and carefully draw over the back of the pencil design so that a faint outline of the design is transferred to the card. If necessary, make this bolder using a marker pen. Cut out the template.

Note
The cakes in this book are all 20 cm (8") wide and 7.5 cm (3") deep. The template shapes provided have all been reproduced at half their actual size. Before copying any of the templates, enlarge the design to the right size (20 × 7.5 cm/8 × 3") using a photocopier.

Enlarging and Reducing

Cakes come in all shapes and sizes and it is vital to know how to enlarge and reduce master designs so that the template fits the cake sides. For example, a tiered cake should have the same pattern on the sides of each cake, but the pattern should be scaled to the size of each. Cake sides are usually of the same depth, so the following method effectively elongates or shortens the width of the design. The instructions given here are for straight-sided cakes, where the sides are of equal length. If the cake has sides of unequal length (for example, extended octagonal or rectangular shapes), treat each side of differing length individually and produce a separate grid for each.

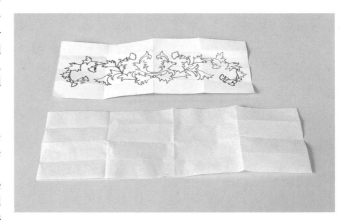

1 To enlarge a design, carefully trace the chosen design on to a piece of paper 20 × 7.5 cm (8 × 3"), keeping the design central on the paper. Define the trace marks with a pen or marker. Cut a piece of greaseproof paper to the size of your cake side. Fold in half from left to right; repeat, making four equal sections. Then fold in half from top to bottom and repeat, also making four equal sections. This is the greaseproof paper grid. Fold the original 20 × 7.5 cm (8 × 3") design the same way. Unfold the greaseproof grid and original design; each will be divided into 16 equal sections.

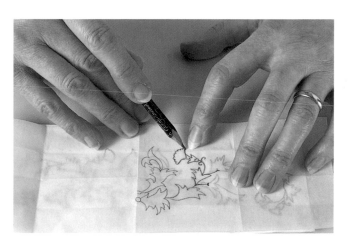

2 Place the greaseproof grid over the original design lining up the centre marks and begin to trace through the design with a pencil, starting from the centre and moving towards the right. Move the greaseproof paper grid to the left slightly and continue tracing.

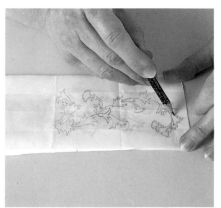

3 Continue in this way until one half of the design has been copied on to the greaseproof grid.

4 Where designs are symmetrical, simply refold the greaseproof grid in half (with the graphite lines outermost), turn over and trace through the design on to the other side of the grid.

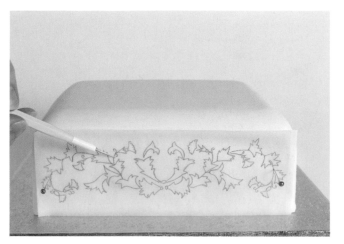

5 Your enlarged template (25.5 × 7.5 cm/10 × 3″) is now complete. Attach to the cake with glass-headed dressmakers' pins, making sure that any pin holes will be covered by the finished sugarcraft design once the template has been removed. Scribe the design through the template on to the surface of the cake.

Note

*To reduce a design, follow Step 1, but in Step 2 move the paper grid to the **right** and continue tracing. Follow the remaining steps.*

Templates for Curved Cake Sides

The following instructions can be applied to any cake with curved sides. If you need to enlarge or reduce a design for a curved cake, cut a separate piece of greaseproof paper (baking parchment) the same size as one of the divisions in step 1 and use this as a greaseproof grid (see Enlarging and Reducing Designs, pages 8–9).

1 Cut a strip of greaseproof paper to the circumference of the cake, plus a 2.5 cm (1″) overlap. Fold the overlap in on itself and ignore for now. Decide the number of times you wish to repeat the chosen design around the cake (say, six times), then fold the greaseproof strip into the same number of divisions using a concertina fold for accuracy.

2 Place one division of the greaseproof strip over the master design and trace through. If making a shaped template, refold the concertina strip and cut around the traced outline. If transferring a design pattern, trace on to each division. The master design will be repeated six times around the greaseproof strip. Transfer to card if necessary, and wrap around the cake, pinning one end to the overlap.

PIPING TECHNIQUES

These decorating techniques are used on several cakes in the book. Plain picot edging is also known as dot lace edging.

Diamond Picot Edging

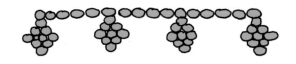

1 *Place a No. 0 piping tube into a small parchment piping bag filled with royal icing. Pipe a row of single small dots to create a base line. Allow to dry.*

2 *On every fifth dot, pipe another single dot and allow to dry.*

3 *Add two more dots to these single dots and allow to dry. To these add a row of three dots, building the edging out away from the cake side. Allow to dry.*

4 *Repeat the process in reverse, decreasing the number of dots on each row and finishing with a single dot to create the diamond effect.*

Plain Picot Edging

1 *Pipe the base line as before, but then pipe groups of three dots, leaving a space between each. Allow to dry. Add two dots to each group of three, building the picot edging away from the cake side, and allow to dry. Complete by adding a single dot to each pair.*

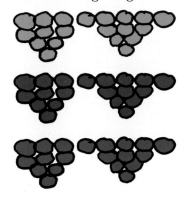

Cutting a Leaf Bag

Several of the cakes that follow require leaf decoration, made using a parchment piping bag (cone) without a tube and with the tip cut to shape.

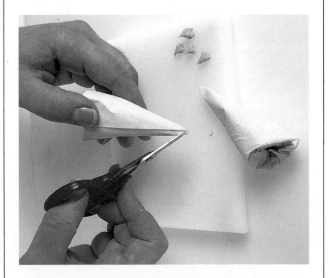

Fill the piping bag with royal icing. Flatten the tip of the bag and cut the tip to form a V-shaped opening with a pair of sharp scissors.

A SHORT GLOSSARY

Off-set work: decorations that have been piped in royal icing, pastillage, gum paste, or whatever, *off* the cake, and allowed to dry before attaching to the cake surface.

Direct piping: decorative piping worked directly on to the cake surface itself.

Overlay: where a template is used as a cutting guide, the cut area of paste being removed to expose the undersurface of the cake.

Inlay: a dry-paste panel which fits within a cut-away area of the cake to form an inset.

Cushion: used in conjunction with appliqué work to give greater depth to the final decoration.

Ribbon insertion: where edible paste ribbons are applied to the cake coating in such a way that they appear to be woven in and out of the rolled fondant (sugarpaste).

Criqué: where portions of cake are removed (usually using a template guide) to form a recess feature.

Note: Gold or Silver Embellishing

When using gold or silver to decorate any part of the cake, ensure that the product is edible. Otherwise, remove any gold or silver painted decoration before serving the cake.

Basic Recipes

The following recipes are all well-tried and tested
and have been used throughout the book.

PURE MEXICAN PASTE

The consistency of Pure Mexican Paste should be elastic when first mixed up. It sets and dries hard and is ideal for off-set pieces where strength is required. All the paste creations in this book have been made with either Pure Mexican Paste or Mexican Paste 2 (see below) and are completely edible.

- *225 g (8 oz/2 cups) icing (confectioners') sugar, sifted*
- *15 ml (3 tsp) gum tragacanth or CMC (carboxymethylcellulose)*
- *30–35 ml (6–7 tsp) cold water*
- *10 ml (2 tsp) liquid glucose*

Sift the icing sugar and gum tragacanth (CMC) together, forming a well in the centre. Add the liquid glucose and 30 ml (6 tsp) of the water and mix all the ingredients together; you may need to add the remaining 5 ml (1 tsp) water if the paste appears to be dry, crumbly or cracking. Knead until all ingredients are well blended.

To store, divide into 3 or 4 portions, double-wrap with plastic – expelling all the air – seal in an airtight container, and keep in a cool place, such as the bottom of the refrigerator, for up to six weeks.

MEXICAN PASTE 2

For a softer set paste that is more pliable to use, follow the recipe and method for Pure Mexican Paste (above) and incorporate an equal quantity of rolled fondant (sugarpaste) or pastello. This more pliable paste is suitable for smocking panels, appliqué work and small off-set pieces.

To store, double-wrap in plastic, seal in an airtight container and keep in a cool place for up to three months or more.

SUGAR GLUE

This standard recipe is used extensively for sticking paste to paste and is not only edible, but palatable too.

- *150 ml (5 fl oz/²/₃ cup) cold water*
- *30 g (1 oz) rolled fondant (sugarpaste), broken into pieces*
- *15 ml (3 tsp) clear alcohol (vodka or white rum)*

Place the water and rolled fondant pieces into a small glass bowl and heat in a microwave for about 30 seconds, until softened. Sieve into another bowl and stir in the vodka or rum. Alternatively, add 150 ml (5 fl oz/²/₃ cup) boiling water to the broken rolled fondant pieces in a heatproof bowl and stir. Place over a pan of boiling water and continue stirring until all the fondant pieces have melted. Sieve as above, then add vodka or rum. Transfer to a jar, seal and store in a cool place or in the bottom of the refrigerator as long as needed.

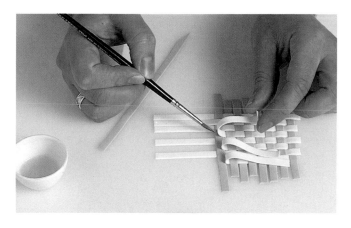

STRONGER GLUE

This adhesive is used for gluing together separate petals and sticking together off-set pieces before attaching to the cake. Note that dry off-set items are always attached to the cake with royal icing and not sugar glue.

- *15 ml (3 tsp) tepid water*
- *5 ml (1 tsp) gum tragacanth (or CMC)*

Pour the water into a cup, then sprinkle the gum tragacanth on to the water and whisk vigorously. It will become thick within seconds. If it is too thick, add a few more drops of water. It can be stored in a small bottle in the refrigerator for a few weeks.

ROYAL ICING 1

It is essential that all equipment used should be scalded with hot water and washing up liquid (detergent) before beginning.

- *25 ml (5 tsp) egg white substitute (albumen) powder*
- *150 ml (5 fl oz/2/3 cup) cold water*
- *680 g (1½ lb/6 cups) icing (confectioners') sugar, sifted*

Whisk the egg white powder and water together and sieve; this becomes your egg white solution. Put into a machine mixing bowl with the icing sugar, keeping back 10–15 ml (2–3 tsp); it is easier to add more sugar than to make more solution to gain the right consistency. Using an electric mixer with a beater attachment, mix on a low speed to incorporate the icing sugar – it should be soft and shiny at this stage. Then beat on medium speed for 3–5 minutes. It is impossible to overbeat royal icing, as it can be stirred back down to remove any excess air which may have been incorporated.

To test that the icing is ready, pull a palette knife (spatula) through the mixture and lift out a small quantity; this should form a firm peak. If the consistency is too soft, either beat in the remaining icing sugar or continue to beat the mixture for a few more minutes.

To store, scrape down the bowl sides so that they are free from icing, push either cling film (plastic wrap) or a plastic bag on to the surface of the royal icing and cover with a damp cloth. Alternatively, place mixture in an airtight container. Do not store in the refrigerator, but keep in a cool place. To revive the icing, simply re-beat on medium speed.

ROYAL ICING 2

If egg white substitute (albumen) powder is hard to find, use this alternative recipe. Also use for off-set items for added strength.

- *2 large egg whites*
- *450 g (1 lb/4 cups) icing (confectioners') sugar, sifted*

If using an electric mixer, place the egg whites in a bowl and whisk on medium speed until frothy. Change to the beater attachment, then gradually add the icing sugar until the desired consistency is achieved. The icing is ready when peaks have formed. If the royal icing is too firm it may be let down with the addition of a little more egg white. Store as for Royal Icing 1.

Side Design Projects

So often the tops of cakes are beautifully ornamented with flower sprays or piped work, for example, and yet the sides appear comparatively bare. Therefore, whether you are a newcomer to cake decorating or experienced in the art of sugarwork, the following projects have been designed to illustrate and instruct in the many varied decorative techniques that can be applied to cake sides. The techniques vary in complexity: the simpler projects appear first, increasing in difficulty as the book – and your skills – progress. Nearly all the projects, however, require a sound knowledge of preparing templates, so do read the section on Basic Techniques carefully before you turn to the following pages. Remember: all the templates shown here have been reproduced at half their original size (20 × 7.5 cm/8 × 3″) and they must be enlarged before copying for use. Finally, since the whole object of the book is to highlight side designs, note that the finished cakes appear with quite plain tops so as not to detract from the side work. However, if you choose one of these designs for a presentation cake, do continue the theme of the decoration over the whole cake for a truly spectacular finish.

Panelled Daisy Cake

When planning side designs for any shape cake the pattern can be laid out in one of two ways, either as a continuous band or as blocks of pattern interspersed with free spaces. A simple and attractive way of enhancing the latter is to highlight the free spaces with line work piped around each area of design. This technique looks most effective when more than one block of designs is visible from a distance.

'Panelling' is the name given to this style of side design work. There are two main types of panelling, usually referred to as closed and open. 'Closed' panels are completely surrounded by piped line work and 'open' panels have at least one side of the line work omitted. For this panelled cake with a daisy design I have chosen a 20 cm (8″) square cake decorated with two open panels on each side.

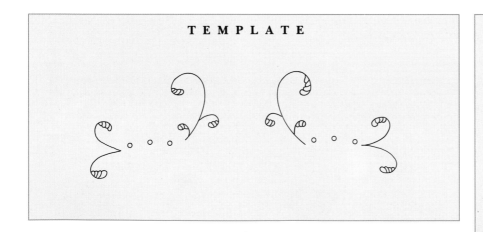

TEMPLATE

REQUIREMENTS

- *20 cm (8″) square cake coated with 900 g (2 lb) marzipan and allowed to dry for 24 hours*
- *900 g (2 lb) rolled fondant (sugarpaste)*
- *cake tilter*
- *edible food colours: brown, pale green, cream*
- *greaseproof paper (baking parchment) template*
- *glass-headed dressmakers' pins*
- *scriber*
- *parchment piping bags (cones)*
- *No. 0, 1, 2 writing tubes and No. 5 shell tube*
- *royal icing*
- *24 daisies for cake sides made from Mexican Paste and allowed to set*

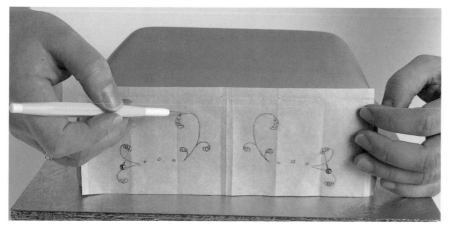

1 Colour the rolled fondant brown and cover the cake in the usual way, leaving it to dry for approximately 24 hours. Cut a greaseproof paper template to fit one of your cake sides and fold in half. Copy the daisy and panel line design on to one half of the template, refold and trace through on to the other half, ensuring that the graphite lines are on the same face of your greaseproof paper. Pin the template into position, then transfer the main lines of the flower foliage on to the cake coating by scribing through the greaseproof paper. Mark the flower positions with a dot. Do *not* scribe the panel work lines, simply mark the top and bottom of each line – the piping will automatically fall in the right position.

2 Fill a small parchment piping bag containing a No. 1 piping tube with pale green royal icing. Pull the end of the tube along the scribed lines and pressure out the royal icing to form the stems and feathered foliage.

3 Fill a small parchment bag containing a No. 2 piping tube with cream-coloured royal icing. Attach the icing to one of the upper marks of the panel section and, moving the tip of the tube out away from the cake side, pipe a vertical line down one side of the panel to the corresponding lower mark. Gravity will pull the line straight down the side of your cake. Complete all the vertical lines the same way. Continue with the same tube and pipe the loops between the tops of the vertical lines on each panel, touching the tip of the tube to the cake coating at the beginning and end of each loop. Gravity will pull your loops to the correct position, but care must be taken that each loop is of the same size.

4 Repeat these lines using a No. 1 piping tube on the inside of the previously piped lines. The distance between the two rows of lines should be equal to the size of the tube's tip. Take a No. 0 tube and pipe a further line inside, giving three lines altogether of decreasing sizes. Then over-pipe the outer No. 2 line with a No. 1 line and again over-pipe with a No. 0 line. Over-pipe the middle No. 1 line with a No. 0 tube. Do not over-pipe the inner No. 0 line.

5 Continue until all the built-up panel lines have been completed. Enhance the panel line loops by piping small dots above the design as shown. Attach the daisies in marked positions with a little royal icing. Pipe a small shell border using a No. 5 piping tube and cream-coloured royal icing. Pipe small leaves over alternate shells using a parchment bag cut to shape containing pale green royal icing (see Basic Techniques, page 11).

VARIATION *This round cake, coated with cream-coloured fondant, demonstrates a different kind of panel work. Here the built-up peach-coloured loops have been piped to form a continuous band around the cake. Peach and white flowers complete the panel design, echoing the larger flower spray mounted on a doily plate covering the top of the cake.*

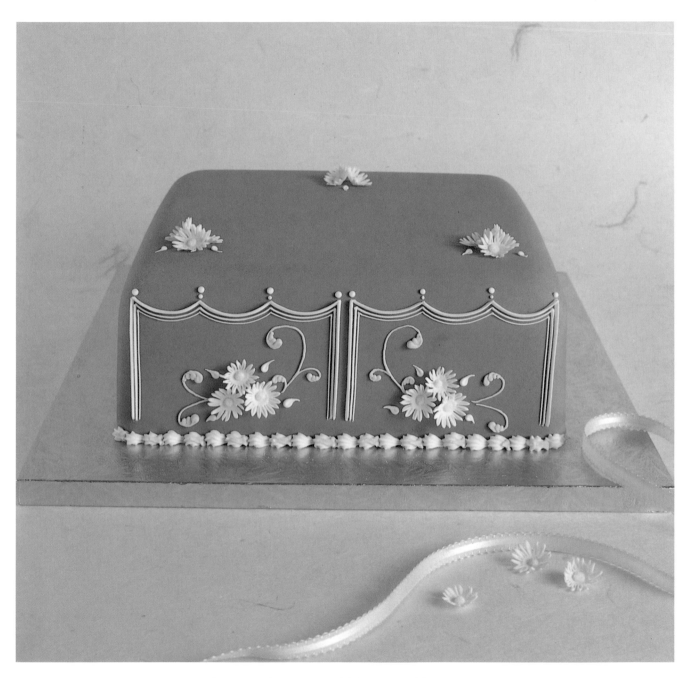

The fresh white daisy sprays and delicate green foliage contrast well with the rich brown fondant cake.

Miniature Smocking

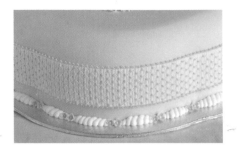

'Smock' is an Anglo-Saxon word meaning shift or chemise. It was originally a plain garment without any gathering. Now, however, when thinking of this technique, one tends to visualize early farmers' garments featuring smocking as a practical finish, rather than for ornament. The material was gathered to form bold, textured panels for protection, rather than for decorative purposes. Children's clothes were often smocked but then embellished with a variety of decorative stitches.

When applied to cake decoration, smocking tends to be time consuming. However, once the design has been marked out and piped with stitches, the completed cake looks very appealing. Take care not to rush the patterns, as evenness is essential for the correct finish.

There are several types of smocking used in cake decorating. To make the smock ridges you will need to use a ribbed rolling pin which gives the perfect base to work on. There are different types of ribbed rolling pins, either with grooves running in bands around the pin, or lines of grooves running the length of the rolling pin. The finer these grooves, the finer the smocking panels will be. Here I have used a very fine ribbed roller producing grooved lines suitable for the application of miniature smocking.

REQUIREMENTS

- 20 cm (8") scalloped oval cake coated with 800 g (1¾ lb) marzipan
- 900 g (2 lb) rolled fondant (sugarpaste)
- edible food colours: pale pink, mint green, turquoise blue
- greaseproof paper (baking parchment) and cardboard for templates
- cake tilter
- glass-headed dressmakers' pins
- scriber
- sugar glue
- paintbrush
- Mexican Paste 2
- smocking pin
- fine, smooth-bladed vegetable knife
- round-ended tweezers or spring hair grip
- royal icing
- parchment piping bags (cones)
- No. 00, 0 and 3 piping tubes
- tiny plunger blossoms in aqua

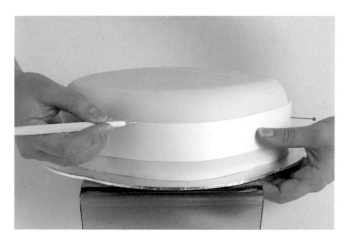

1 Colour the rolled fondant pale pink and cover the cake in the usual way, allowing it to dry for 24 hours. Measure the circumference of cake with a strip of greaseproof paper. Fold in half and, using it as a guide for length, cut a strip of cardboard 3.75 cm (½″) wide. Place this against the cake half way up the side and secure with glass-headed dressmakers' pins. Using a scriber, carefully mark the top and bottom of the cardboard template; remove and repeat on the opposite side of the cake. Paint this area with a little sugar glue.

2 Using Mexican Paste 2, roll out a rectangle, at least twice as wide as the cardboard template, and at least half as long as the circumference of the cake. With your smocking pin, roll across the paste firmly and evenly. Place the cardboard template over the paste and cut out two strips of paste, keeping them together. Remove excess paste and place in a plastic bag to prevent drying.

Take care when applying the paste band to the side of the cake not to distort the fine ribbed effect. When one strip has been attached, paint the ends of the strip with a little sugar glue, then apply the second strip, butting-up the joins.

3 Using a pair of round-ended tweezers or a spring hair grip, carefully pinch the ribs of paste together to form the base of the smocking panel. Repeat along the ribbed lines all the way round the cake, working from left to right, building up a diamond-shaped pattern as shown. As these ribbed lines are fine and close, the pinched pattern will need to be kept small and delicate.

4 Colour a small quantity of royal icing with a mixture of mint green and turquoise blue food colours to make a soft aqua tint. Place in a small parchment piping bag with a No. 0 writing tube. Colour an equal quantity of royal icing pale pink and place in a small parchment piping bag with a No. 00 writing tube. With the aqua icing and following the diamond pattern, pipe a line from the nipped paste on one line to the nipped paste on the line below. Continue around the band of paste in the same way. With the pale pink icing, pipe two tiny lines across the nipped sections to give the effect of a continuous pattern. Repeat this all the way round the band of paste.

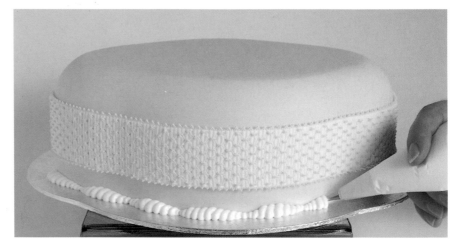

5 Complete the band by piping a small plain picot edge (see Basic Techniques, page 10) along the top and bottom edges of the band with a No. 0 tube and the aqua-coloured royal icing. Pipe a rope border with a No. 3 tube and white royal icing.

VARIATION *This unusual fan-shaped cake has been covered with ivory-coloured rolled fondant, then decorated with a shaped band of miniature smocking. The piped smocking is in rose pink and pale green and the top edge of the band is decorated with off-set lace pieces dusted in deep pink.*

Tiny plunger blossoms, in a deeper shade of aqua, enhance the finished cake.

Leaf Cascade

Leaf cutters and a few flowers are all you need to create this delicate side design. If you cannot find the right cutters use a cardboard template. Whichever technique you choose, shapes can be cut and softened by frilling to create a cascade of shaded colour.

REQUIREMENTS

- 20 cm (8") petal cake coated with 800 g (1¾ lb) marzipan and allowed to dry for 24 hours
- 900 g (2 lb) rolled fondant (sugarpaste)
- edible food colours: peach, brown
- Mexican Paste 2, divided into two and one portion coloured peach
- fine-bladed palette knife (spatula)
- rose-leaf cutter set or cardboard templates
- polythene (plastic) sheet
- paintbrushes
- edible dusting colour: apple green
- cocktail sticks (toothpicks)
- parchment piping bags (cones)
- royal icing
- No. 0 and 2 piping tubes
- cake tilter
- sugar glue
- primula flowers (non-wired)

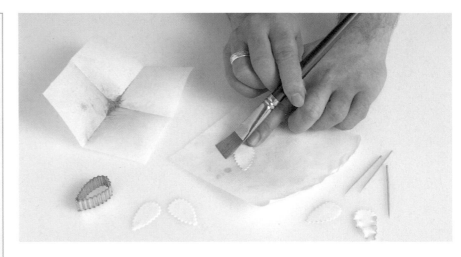

1 To prepare the cake, colour the rolled fondant peach, cover the cake and leave to dry for 24 hours. To make the leaves, roll out some white Mexican Paste thinly so if a fine-bladed palette knife is passed beneath the paste it can just be seen. Using the medium-sized rose-leaf cutter, cut out six leaves. Cover all except one with a sheet of polythene. Load a wide flat brush with apple-green dusting powder and wipe the sides of the bristles over the edge of paste, working from the outside of the leaf in towards the middle. The colour should be picked up just on the leaf edge. Soften the two sides of the leaf *only* by rolling and frilling with a cocktail stick. Colour and shape the remaining leaves in this way.

2 Fill a small parchment piping bag with royal icing and attach a No. 2 piping tube and pipe a snail's-trail border around the base of the cake and allow to dry. Attach one leaf to the middle of each scallop shape over the lower border of the cake with a little sugar glue.

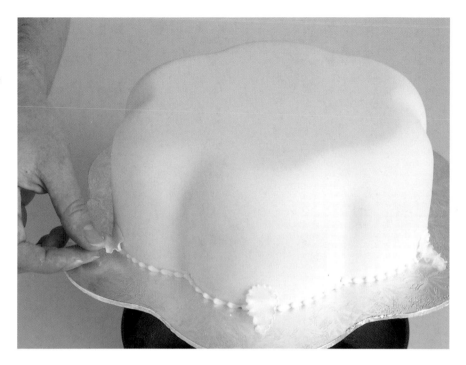

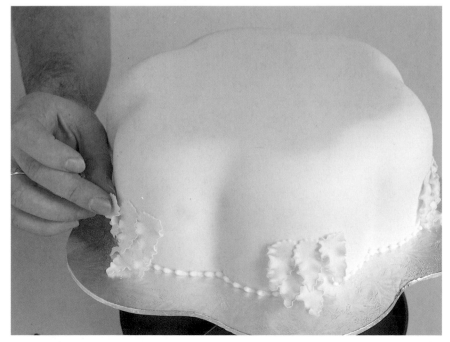

3 For the second layer of leaves, add a small quantity of peach-coloured Mexican Paste 2 to the remaining white Mexican Paste 2. Using the same sized cutter, cut out 12 leaves, dust with colour and frill as before. Attach two leaves to the middle of each scallop shape slightly higher on the cake side so they hang down and overlap the first layer. For the third layer of leaves, add another small quantity of peach-coloured Mexican Paste 2 to the pale Mexican Paste 2 already mixed. Repeat the same method as described before but this time use a slightly smaller rose-leaf cutter. Cut out 18 leaves (3 for each scallop), and colour and frill as before. Once again, attach the leaves slightly higher on the cake side so they hang down and overlap the second layer.

4 Continue in this way using the smaller leaf cutter. Make each subsequent layer of petals slightly darker peach and attach each row slightly higher on the side of the cake. You will need a total of 30 leaves for row four (five for each scallop), and 36 leaves for rows five and six (six for each scallop). For the last row of leaves, frill around the entire shape.

5 Position small sprays of frilly peach primulas at the top of each indent, securing with royal icing.

VARIATION *This teardrop-shaped wedding cake demonstrates the same layered cascade effect, made with varying sizes of petal cutters and featuring a stronger use of gradated colour.*

Complete the overall design by piping fine freehand embroidery in brown- and peach-coloured royal icing with a No. 0 writing tube.

Crimping

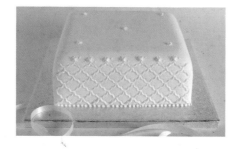

Crimping is carried out on cakes freshly covered with rolled fondant (sugarpaste). It is imperative that the work is completed before the cake covering starts to skin over, otherwise the patterns will be marred by cracking. To retard skinning, cover the cake with a polythene (plastic) sheet.

This technique employs a specialized tool. Crimpers are not new – they have been used in the bakery industry for generations, and were first known as 'nippers'. These tools, of which many types are sold, come in a variety of patterns and sizes ranging from 1 cm (¼″) up to 5 cm (2″) wide. Crimpers work on a spring hinge movement with the distance between the crimper blades governing the amount of rolled fondant that will be patterned. The blades fall into two categories: closed-bladed crimpers, where the blade patterns are parallel to each other, giving a finely pinched ridge of fondant; and open-bladed crimpers, where the blade patterns are mirror images of each other, giving a much bolder crimp. They can be used together or on their own. For the design on this 20 cm (8″) square cake I have used a closed-bladed crimper.

REQUIREMENTS

- *20 cm (8″) square cake coated with 900 g (2 lb) marzipan and allowed to dry for 24 hours*
- *900 g (2 lb) rolled fondant (sugarpaste)*
- *greaseproof paper (baking parchment) and cardboard for template*
- *cake tilter*
- *scriber*
- *1.75 cm (¾″) double-scalloped crimper*
- *edible food colours: green, yellow*
- *Mexican Paste 2*
- *small plunger blossom cutter*
- *royal icing*
- *No. 1 and 2 piping tubes*

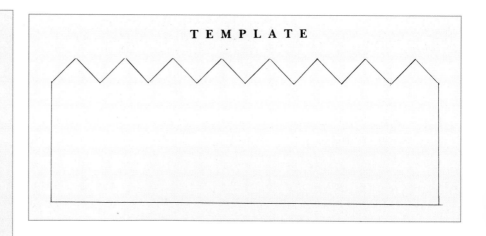

TEMPLATE

1 Before coating the cake with rolled fondant, copy the small 'V' design on to a piece of greaseproof paper cut to the same size as the cake side with a small allowance so that the template still fits once the cake has been coated. Transfer the design and cut a cardboard template (see Basic Techniques, page 8).

Coat the cake with rolled fondant and remove excess paste in the usual way. Before the coating starts to skin over, position the cardboard template against the cake side and very gently scribe the pattern on to the soft fondant. The design needs to be marked only along the top of the cake side, not all the way down. Repeat on all sides. Remove the template before crimping.

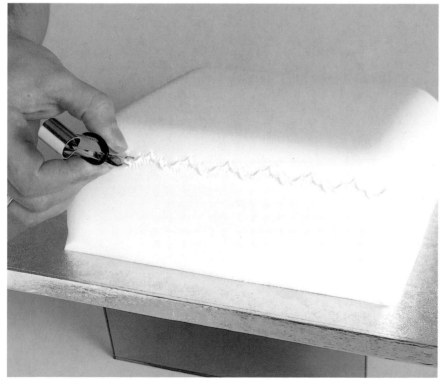

2 Until you are proficient at crimping, wrap an elastic band around the middle of the crimper to restrict the hinge movement. Hold a 1.75 cm (¾″) double-scalloped crimper in one hand with the ends slightly apart, so the patterned blades are at right angles to the cake surface. Twist the crimper round so that the blades are in line with the scribed design. Begin crimping the first part of the 'V' pattern by pushing the slightly open blades a little way into the soft fondant, then bring one blade towards the other, pinching the fondant between. Slightly release the pressure on the crimper blades, just enough to remove the crimper tool from the coating. Once the blades are clear of the cake, release the pressure completely. Reposition the crimper and repeat the action to form the second side of the 'V' pattern. Continue this way, following the scribed design all around the top of the four cake sides.

3 Once the first row has been completed proceed by crimping down the cake sides creating a diamond pattern as shown. Beware: if care is not taken problems may occur. Over-crimping happens when the blades are either too far apart on contact with the fondant, or too tightly pinched together. Under-crimping occurs when insufficient pressure is applied to the blades, which results in the crimper work looking undefined.

4 Pipe a small shell border in green royal icing using a No. 2 piping tube.

5 To complete the cake, using Mexican Paste 2, coloured yellow, make approximately 25 tiny plunger blossom flowers for each side and allow to set. Apply clusters of tiny blossom flowers, attaching them to the cake with royal icing, and finish with green royal icing leaves piped with a No. 1 piping tube.

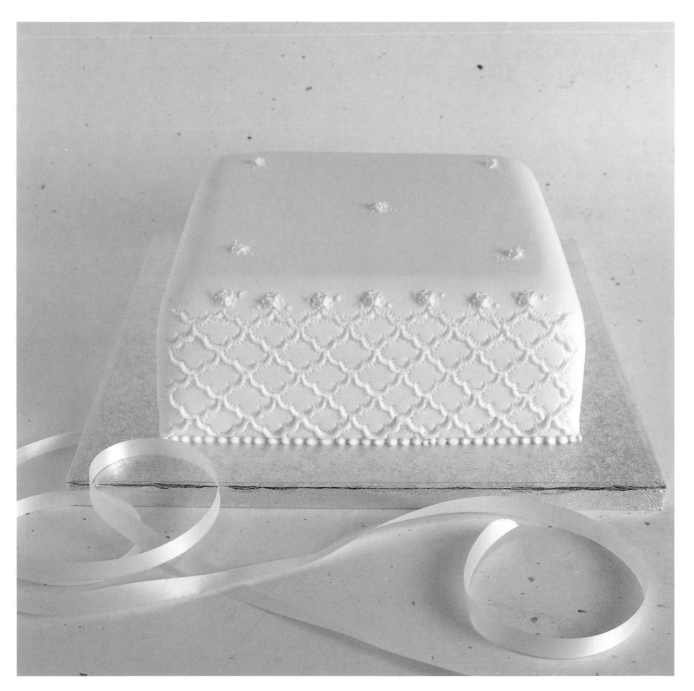

Crimping is an effective side decoration for a simple celebration or christening cake.

Embossing

The art of embossing has been in existence for centuries. Native Americans used embossers to adorn their leather work, a technique used worldwide to this day, and one which readily adapts to rolled fondant (sugarpaste).

Embossing tools – or buttons as they are sometimes called – are small plates of varying shapes and sizes with a patterned relief surface. Choose an embosser where the marker lines stand proud of the background. As with crimping work it is important to complete all patterning before the rolled fondant (sugarpaste) begins to skin over.

This embossed cake has been coated with cream fondant, cut and moulded so that it represents gift wrapping. A sponge was dipped in diluted green food colour and then gently daubed over the top and sides of the soft fondant to create a mottled effect. A rosebud embossing tool was used to create the pattern. The red rosebuds and dark green leaves were painted once the cake had been allowed to dry.

The ribbons were made from dark green Mexican Paste 2 and attached to the cake with a little sugar glue. The ribbon was painted with gold lustre and then glossed with confectioners' varnish. A No. 2 tube was used to create the tiny shell border at the base of the cake.

Modelled Border Design

Border patterns can be as plain and simple as you wish, or as diverse and intricate as your skills allow. Piping borders with royal icing is the first thing which springs to mind with this subject, creating shells, rope and boat scrolls, using either a plain or toothed tube. These are the more popular types of borders, being quick and easily executed, with colour added to suit the particular cake design. Many different variations can be achieved with practice, simply by over-piping with different sizes of piping tubes.

Other borders may be created by combining coloured pastes which may be moulded and modelled into shape or cut into strips. These borders can then be applied to the cake using a little sugar glue or royal icing. Small rounds of paste can be moulded and used whole or cut in half; strips of paste can be used flat or rolled and curled and then applied; long rolled ropes of pastes in co-ordinating colours may be used singly or twisted together to form candy stripes or plaited (braided), and placed around the base of the cake. These paste borders may be left as they are or further enhanced with crimpers or embossing tools. The possibilities are endless.

For this children's cake I have used modelled Mexican Paste 2 to create the border design. To give further scope for design, the border has been extended not only up the cake side but on to the cake-board as well. The theme is taken from a nursery wallpaper – recognizable by even the youngest birthday recipient – but, of course, this idea can be developed for adults using a different subject, such as cut-out stamps and piped franking marks for a philatelist.

TEMPLATE

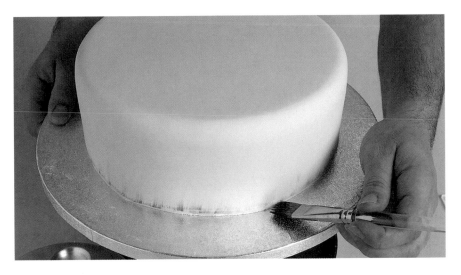

1 Colour the rolled fondant with turquoise blue food colour. Coat your cake in the normal way and allow to set for 24 hours. Apply dark green liquid food colour to the base of the cake to create a background for the grass stems.

2 Colour one quantity of royal icing with gooseberry- or moss-green food colour and spread over the cakeboard. Using a dry, firm pastry brush, stipple the green icing, dabbing the lower portion of the cake and covering the join at the base. Before the icing starts to set, apply patches of royal icing coloured with yellow and brown food colours to add depth, working into the textured surface with the dry pastry brush. Fill three parchment piping bags with the moss-green, yellow and brown food colours and cut a fine hole in the end of each. Pipe bands of grass and foliage up the lower portion of the cake side.

3 With Mexican Paste 2, colour and mould a selection of varying sizes of toadstools and mushrooms, ladybirds, frogs, snails, rocks and stones, hedgehogs, flowers, milestones, fence posts, ivy leaves and so on. Remember to keep these moulded items small and in perspective since they will be used on the lower part of the cake and should not overpower the cake or top ornament. Leave to set to make them easier to handle. Paint the fine details with food colours let down with clear alcohol and enhance each with appropriately coloured dusting colours. First attach the background items – such as the fence posts and milestones – with the green royal icing.

4 Continue adding the modelled decorations to the cakeboard and sides, working from the background to the foreground, to build up a three-dimensional picture border.

5 Fill a small parchment piping bag with white royal icing and fit a No. 0 writing tube. Pipe freehand curves, gliding the tube tip over the blue fondant surface, to represent cloud formations or use the template provided. Using the same bag, enhance these shapes by gently pressuring out the icing with a slight rotation of the tube. The clouds should appear bolder in the middle than at the sides. Colour a small quantity of royal icing with black food colour and pipe pairs of tiny scallop shapes between the clouds to represent birds flying in the distance.

The finished cake is a perfect centrepiece for a child's birthday celebration.

Cutter Inlay Cake

Inlay work on the top or sides gives a new perspective to a cake, creating depth and character. These panels may be used any way you choose, making perfect areas for small run-outs, appliqué flowers, badges, paintings and motifs of any type to match the overall cake design. For this 21st birthday cake I have chosen a cricket theme, and introduced a paste-weaving technique for the panels.

REQUIREMENTS

- *20 cm (8″) hexagonal cake coated with 900 g (2 lb) marzipan and allowed to dry for 24 hours*
- *900 g (2 lb) rolled fondant (sugarpaste)*
- *edible food colours: cream, dark brown, red, pale green, yellow, black*
- *clear alcohol, such as vodka*
- *paintbrushes*
- *cake tilter*
- *5 cm (2″) oval cutter*
- *Mexican Paste 2*
- *mint cutter*
- *polythene (plastic) sheet*
- *sugar glue*
- *royal icing*
- *parchment piping bags (cones)*
- *No. 00, 1 and 2 piping tubes*

1 To prepare the cake, colour the rolled fondant pale green. Paint the marzipan with a clear alcohol, omitting the areas which will be cut out. Since the exact position of the inlays is not known, do not be too liberal with the alcohol. Small markers on the cakeboard at the bottom of the cake help position the cutter once the rolled fondant has been applied. Coat the cake with the pale green fondant, position the cutter on the side of cake as shown and push it into the soft cake coating. Remove the paste from within cutter, then remove the cutter. Repeat on each side. Leave to set for approximately 24 hours.

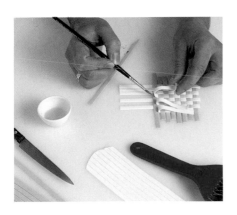

2 To make inlay panels, colour a small quantity of Mexican Paste 2 light brown using a dash of cream food colour mixed with dark brown. Colour an equal quantity of Mexican Paste 2 cream. Roll both the brown- and cream-coloured pastes thinly, ensuring they are the same thickness. Cut each sheet of paste into strips using a mint cutter. Place under a polythene sheet to prevent the paste forming a crust. Position the cream strips of paste to form the 'warp' weave. Apply a little sugar glue to one end of alternate strips. Lift non-glued strips and place one piece of brown paste across the glued area of the cream 'warp' weave to form the brown 'weft' weave. Reposition the cream strips. Bend the other alternate strips of cream paste forwards over the face of the interwoven area and apply a little sugar glue to their under surfaces. Place a second strip of brown 'weft' weave in line with the first and reposition the cream 'warp' weave.

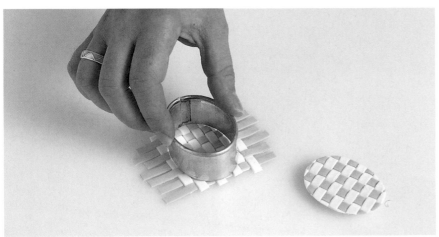

3 Continue in this way – lifting alternate strips of cream paste, gluing and positioning brown strips – until the cutter fits comfortably over the interwoven area. Cut 6 panels and leave to dry.

4 Apply a little royal icing to the exposed areas of marzipan on the cake sides and position the inlay panels in the cut-away areas.

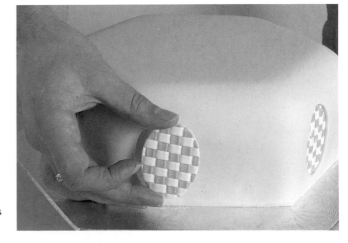

5 Mould 6 cricket bats using Mexican Paste 2. Paint the handle detail in with black food colour. Using red compound, colour a small quantity of Mexican Paste 2 and mould 3 balls. Cut each in half and leave to dry. Pipe the stitching in yellow royal icing using a No. 00 tube. Position the bats and balls on the inlay panels and attach with a little royal icing. To make the score cards, thinly roll out a small quantity of white Mexican Paste 2 and cut out 12 squares, each 2 × 2 cm (¾ × ¾"). Allow to dry before painting on the age details with black food colour. Apply to the cake with a little royal icing.

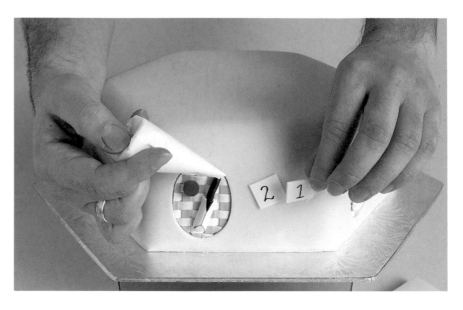

6 Pipe a fine beaded border around the inlay sections using a No. 1 piping tube and mid-brown royal icing.

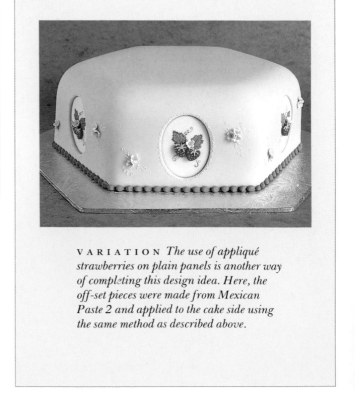

VARIATION *The use of appliqué strawberries on plain panels is another way of completing this design idea. Here, the off-set pieces were made from Mexican Paste 2 and applied to the cake side using the same method as described above.*

To complete the cake, repeat the inlay border design as a gradated dot border at the
base of the cake using a No. 2 piping tube. The cake shown here is hexagonal,
but remember that when working on a curved-sided cake, the inlay panels must be cut
and dried over a curve the same shape as the cake, such as the pan the cake was baked in.
The panels, once dry, can then be painted or decorated before being inserted inside
the cut-away areas. It is best to restrict the size of the cutter used
when working on a curved-sided cake.

Ribbon Insertion

This style of cake decoration derives from the craft of milliners and dressmakers, who add texture and colour to hats or other garments by gathering and stitching continuous sections of ribbon into position to form a series of loops.

Cake decorators have adapted this method by taking small sections of fabric ribbon and pushing both ends into the cake surface to produce a pattern of loops that look as if they have been threaded through the cake coating. This subject has created some controversy within the food industry, but seems to be an accepted practice, providing the cake's recipient knows that the ribbons – being non-edible – must be removed before serving. However, there is an alternative way of making loops using Mexican paste. This method is illustrated here, creating a dramatic – and completely edible – effect on this black-coated cake.

REQUIREMENTS

- 20 cm (8") square cake coated with 900 g (2 lb) marzipan and allowed to dry for 24 hours
- greaseproof paper (baking parchment) and cardboard for template
- dowel rods
- Pure Mexican Paste
- mint cutter or craft knife
- edible food colours: black, red
- edible gold powder or lustre
- clear alcohol, such as vodka
- paintbrushes
- 900 g (2 lb) rolled fondant (sugarpaste)
- cake tilter
- scriber
- royal icing
- parchment piping bag (cone)
- run-out theatrical face masks
- rolled fondant (sugarpaste) for border
- sugar glue

Note
All gold-coloured decorations must be removed from the cake before serving.

1 To make ribbon loops, cut a narrow strip of greaseproof paper for the ribbon template and decide the length of each loop by placing the paper strip over a curved surface, such as a dowel rod, miniature rolling pin or plastic curve. Cut the template to the desired length; the strip should not be too wide or the loops will look heavy. Roll out white Mexican Paste quite thinly and cut strips of paste to the same width and length as the paper template using a mint cutter or craft knife. Repeat using red Mexican Paste. Place each loop over the chosen curve and leave in a warm dry place for several hours to dry. When dry, paint some of the loops with the gold powder mixed with a little clear alcohol.

2 To make the ribbon twists, cut strips of red Mexican Paste using a mint cutter, then cut in half again lengthwise. Cut the strips to the required length, twist as shown and allow to dry.

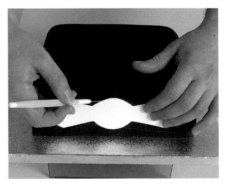

TEMPLATE

3 To prepare the cake, colour the rolled fondant black, cover the cake and leave to dry for 24 hours. Cut a greaseproof paper template to fit the side of your cake, trace the pattern outline from the design given and transfer to cardboard. Cut out the template and gently scribe around the template on to the cake side.

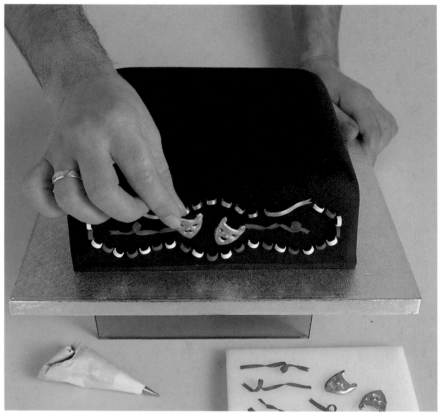

4 Attach the ribbon loops to the cake, aligning the ends of the loops with the lightly scribed line. Use a small amount of royal icing to fix the loops on to the rolled fondant. Alternatively, make small insertions in the cake covering with a craft knife at each end of the ribbon loop, pushing each into the insertion slits to hold. However, care must be taken when applying this technique since the paste loops are fragile and may break. It is important to secure each paste loop well.

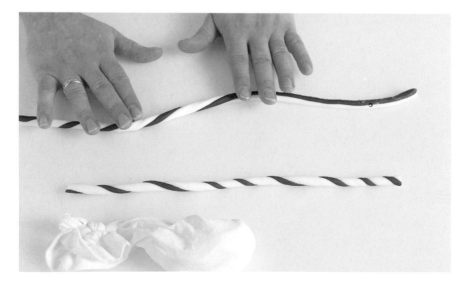

5 Attach the run-out theatrical face masks – painted with gold powder mixed with a little clear alcohol – and the ribbon twists to the cake side with a little royal icing.

6 For the base border, roll two long fingers of fondant, one black and the other white. These should be the same thickness and long enough to go round the cake at least one and a half times. Gently twist the two fondant pieces together, keeping the patterning even. Trim one end neatly.

*To finish, apply a band of sugar glue round the base of the cake, and beginning with
the trimmed end at the back of the cake position the fondant twist at the cake base
and ease round the cake to form a border. Do not stretch the pattern out of shape.
Slightly overlap the fondant twist at the back of the cake, then cut through both strips
so that a neat join is created without any overlap.*

Christmas Cake with Appliqué

The word 'appliqué' originates from France, and is usually applied to needlework, meaning to sew or fasten one piece of material to another. Cake decorators have adapted this technique by cutting out pieces of paste and attaching them to the cake sides or top. Appliqué, as a style of decoration, lends itself to bright colours and bold designs.

The cake I have chosen here has a festive design with a seasonal garland of miniature poinsettias, Christmas roses, pine cones, candy canes, ivy and holly leaves and berries. The appliqué pieces are attached to a base cushion to give more of a relief effect to the cake side than is usually seen in this style of decorating.

REQUIREMENTS

- 20 cm (8") round cake coated with 800 g (1¾ lb) marzipan and allowed to dry for 24 hours
- 900 g (2 lb) rolled fondant (sugarpaste)
- greaseproof paper (baking parchment) for template
- glass-headed dressmakers' pins
- cake tilter
- scriber
- sugar glue

- Mexican Paste 2 for appliqué items
- plunger blossom cutter
- edible food colours: various
- royal icing
- parchment piping bags (cones)
- No. 42 and 0 piping tubes
- holly and ivy cutters
- selection of paintbrushes
- edible dusting powders: various
- polythene (plastic) sheet

MAKING THE APPLIQUÉ DECORATIONS

Use Mexican Paste 2 for the appliqué decorations. Make the miniature Christmas roses with a plunger blossom cutter and the poinsettias with a mini calyx cutter and ball tool; use a small piping bag with a No. 0 tube and yellow royal icing for the stamens. Mould the pine cones and clip with scissors. Make the candy canes from strips of red and white paste twisted together and shaped.
Use holly and ivy cutters for the foliage and mould the holly berries. Use coloured paste, or paint and dust as appropriate. Keep the holly and ivy leaves under a sheet of plastic until needed so they do not dry out completely. The other pieces can be allowed to set.

1 Cover the marzipan-coated cake with white rolled fondant and allow to dry for approximately 24 hours. Fold a greaseproof paper template to give 6 equal divisions around the cake side (see Basic Techniques, page 10). Pin the template into position and mark the scallops on to the rolled fondant using a sharp implement, such as a scriber or needle tool.

2 Using the trimmings from the fondant coating, model 6 finger-shaped 'cushions', thinner at each end than in the middle, and attach to the scribed lines using a little sugar glue.

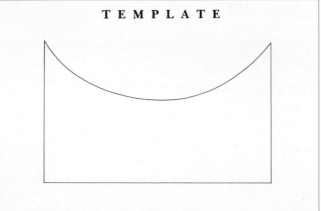

TEMPLATE

3 First position the larger appliqué items, the holly and ivy leaves, and attach to the cushions with royal icing. Apply these pieces while slightly soft.

4 Attach the remaining appliqué pieces, first the pine cones and Christmas roses then the poinsettias, holly berries and candy canes, using royal icing.

5 Fill a large parchment piping bag with a No. 42 tube and pipe a border of small boat scrolls. Make sure that one boat scroll is situated directly beneath the peak of each of the scallops on the cake side.

To finish, position various appliqué pieces into boat scrolls immediately below each scallop peak as shown.

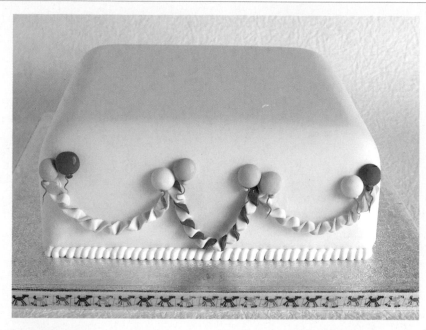

VARIATION *For this children's party cake coated in white rolled fondant, fold a template but only mark the top of each drop with a scriber. It is not necessary to scribe a line to mark each loop, as the paste chains will find their own arc with gravity.*

To complete the cake side mould balloons and strings from Mexican Paste 2 and attach to the rolled fondant coating with a little royal icing. Using a No. 3 plain tube, pipe a continuous rope border around the base of the cake.

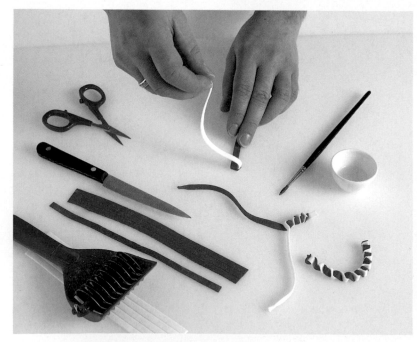

To make the box chain take two complementary coloured strips of Mexican paste 2 and fasten the ends at right angles with sugar glue. (To avoid the Mexican paste 2 drying out and cracking do not cut the strips too long.) Fold at right angles without creasing, laying one strip over the other. Continue bending each strip over its partner, keeping the strips at right angles. Repeat until you have the length you need. Take hold of the ends of the folded paste and pull slightly apart. As the squares open out, a small box chain forms. Attach the chains to the cake using royal icing.

Template Overlay Cake

Template overlay is always carried out on a double rolled fondant (sugarpaste) cake, the first coat being allowed to dry before the second is applied. For the template, use shiny cardboard as it is firm and easy to use on cake sides when cutting a pattern with a craft knife. I have chosen a 20 cm (8") square cake for this template overlay design and have decorated it with miniature appliqué bleeding heart flowers.

REQUIREMENTS

- 20 cm (8") square cake coated with 900 g (2 lb) marzipan and allowed to dry for 24 hours
- 1.8 kg (4 lb) rolled fondant (sugarpaste) divided in half for base and top coats
- edible food colours: cream, pale green and red
- greaseproof paper (baking parchment) and cardboard for templates
- scissors
- clear alcohol, such as vodka
- paintbrushes
- cake tilter
- craft knife
- parchment piping bags (cones)
- No. 0, 1 and two No. 2 piping tubes
- royal icing
- selection of miniature bleeding heart flowers

TEMPLATE

TO PREPARE THE CAKE

Colour 900 g (2 lb) of rolled fondant cream for the base coat and cover the marzipan-coated cake in the normal way, allowing it to dry for approximately 24 hours. Colour the remaining 900 g (2 lb) of rolled fondant pale green for your top coat, cover and leave to one side until required.

Hold the template (see step 2) against the side of the cake and place a marker on the cakeboard where the mid-line of the template is positioned. Then, using clear alcohol, paint the remaining side area.
Note: *it is very important that the template*

remains completely dry, otherwise the top coating of rolled fondant may become marred. For this reason it is advisable to make two identical templates, one to use with the alcohol and the other to use on the top coat. Paint the top and remaining sides in the same way.

Cover the whole cake with the pale green rolled fondant in the usual way, using a smoother to ensure that the top coating is flat against the undercoat. This is very important since there are large areas beneath the green-coloured paste that have no alcohol on them and the two coatings will not be stuck to each other.

51

1 To make the template, cut out a greaseproof paper template the same size as the cake side and fold in half (from left to right) to mark the middle. With a sharp pencil draw one half of the pattern on to one half of the greaseproof template. Trace the other half through to make a true mirror image of the design, ensuring all the graphite lines are on the same face of the greaseproof paper.

2 Place the greaseproof paper template face-down on to a piece of white cardboard and draw firmly over the back of the graphite lines to transfer the overlay template shape on to the card. If necessary emphasize the pattern clearly on the cardboard with a pen. Mark the mid-line on the card template. Carefully cut out with a pair of sharp scissors. When the template has been cut out you will have two portions. One will resemble a bridge span; discard this and use the remaining portion for the template.

3 Place the cardboard template against the cake side in the same position as before, keeping the centre aligned with the marker on the cakeboard. Hold the card firmly, but take care not to mark the soft coating. Carefully cut round the outside of the template with a craft knife. Remove the template from the first side, and reposition and cut the remaining sides in the same way.

4 Gently ease out and remove the rolled fondant within each of the template areas. It may be necessary to clean the cut edge with a finger or thumb by wiping along the shaped outline. However, be careful not to push or indent the fondant when doing this. Allow to dry for 24 hours.

5 Apply the fine piped embroidery design, using a No. 0 tube and white royal icing, as shown.

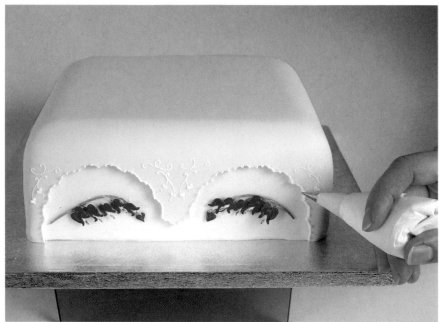

6 Attach sprays of appliqué bleeding heart flowers within the cut-away areas with royal icing.

7 Pipe a picot edge of white dot lace with a No. 1 tube around the overlay shape to create a fine framework.

VARIATION *This wedding cake uses the paste-weaving technique described for the cutter inlay cake (page 38) for the background area. The overlay paste was coloured ivory to complement the deep cream used in the woven sections. Poppies, daisies and maize leaves complete the design.*

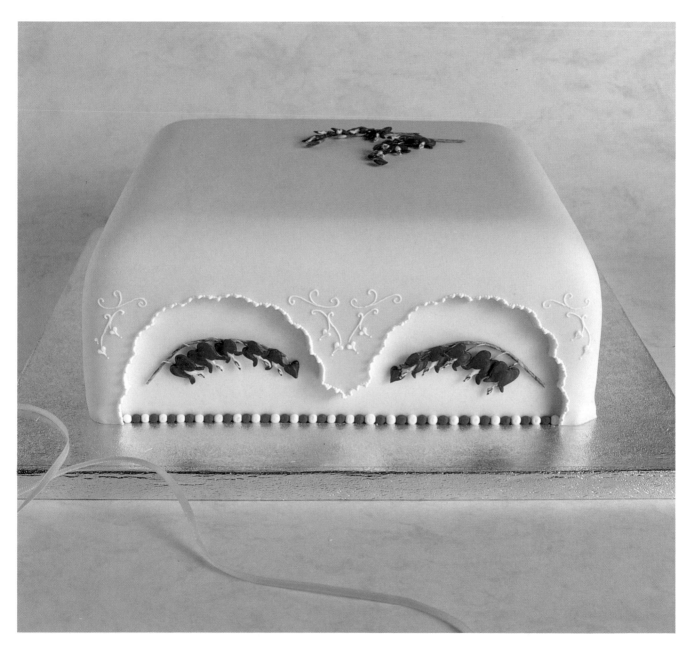

*The cake is finished with a border of alternating red and white bulbs
at the cake base piped with No. 2 tubes.*

Run-Out Motifs

This type of work was first introduced in the 1920s, and it is referred to as flooding, run-in work or, more commonly, as run-out work. This is a very popular technique and the possibilities are endless. For this cake small run-out geese motifs are used to enhance the side decoration on the cake.

REQUIREMENTS

- 20 cm (8") square cake coated with 900 g (2 lb) marzipan and allowed to dry for 24 hours
- greaseproof paper (baking parchment) and white paper for template
- work board or sheet of glass
- waxed paper or Quick Release Sheet (QRS)
- masking tape
- parchment piping bags (cones)
- royal icing
- albumen solution
- No. 1 piping tube
- edible food colours: pale blue, yellow, pale green
- fine sable paintbrush
- anglepoise lamp
- clear alcohol, such as vodka
- edible dusting colours: blue, pink
- feeler gauge
- 900 g (2 lb) rolled fondant (sugarpaste)
- cake tilter
- 20 very small Mexican Paste flowers in various colours

TEMPLATE

56

TO PREPARE ROYAL ICING FOR RUN-OUTS

The consistency of the royal icing is the most important factor to produce good quality run-outs. To obtain a smooth, glossy appearance over the area of the run-out, the royal icing must be far softer in consistency than that used for normal piping. The icing consistency should just hold its shape when piped, but give a smooth and level surface when teased into place with a paintbrush. If the consistency is too soft, the run-out will take longer to dry and the icing may flow over the

borderlines, destroying the piece of work. On the other hand, if the run-out icing is too stiff, it will be very difficult to achieve a picture with a smooth surface.

To obtain the correct consistency, add albumen solution or water to the icing a few drops at a time, allowing it to stand for a while so excess air bubbles collect into pockets. These air bubbles can then be dispersed by gently stirring the icing with a palette knife.

After each addition, make a trail over

the surface of the icing with the mixing implement. Time how long it takes the trail to disappear and for the surface to become level. The correct consistency is when there is no visible sign of the trail and the surface of the icing has become smooth within 10 seconds.

If adding colour to this royal icing, try to avoid making the colours too strong as this tends to destroy the drying quality of the icing and the icing will crumble when removed from the waxed paper.

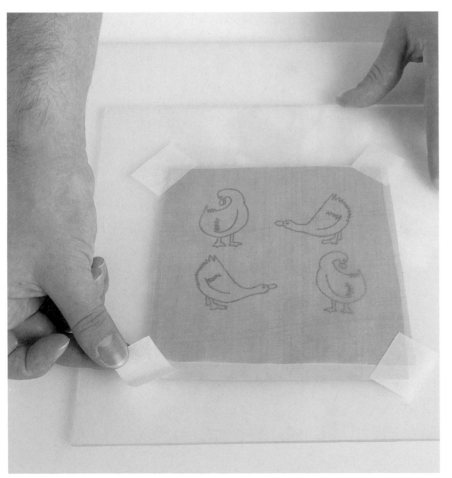

1 Trace the geese (ignoring the flower garlands) on to plain white paper to the correct size, using the enlarging and reducing method if necessary (see Basic Techniques, page 8–9). Place the drawing on a work board or a sheet of glass. Attach a piece of waxed paper or QRS larger than the traced designs to the board or glass with masking tape or small dots of royal icing.

2 Fill a small parchment piping bag with white, normal piping consistency royal icing and attach a No. 1 tube. Fill two more small piping bags, one with yellow and the other with white softened icing – these bags do not need tubes. Have ready a clean soft paintbrush and an anglepoise lamp set up before beginning. Start piping the run-out motif, using the bag containing normal consistency icing to outline the geese.

3 Then, using the parchment piping bags of softened icing, cut a small hole at the tip of each, and start to fill in the picture. Fill in the background portions first, allowing each section to skin under the lamp before filling in the adjacent sections. The geese motifs should have a three-dimensional appearance, giving depth to the picture. Allow to set in a warm, dry place for approximately 24 hours.

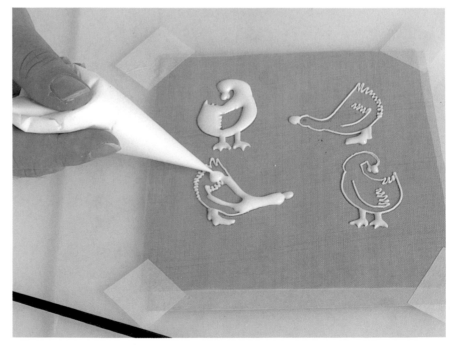

4 Paint the details using food colour let down with clear alcohol or, if wished, dust on colour when the motif is dry. To release the geese from the waxed paper, use either a fine-cranked palette knife or a clean feeler gauge, gently pushing the blade edge under one end of the run-out. Keeping the blade flat to the board, slide it under the motif to the end.

5 To prepare the cake, colour the rolled fondant pale blue, cover the cake as usual and allow to dry for 24 hours. Then, brush the cake sides with blue and pink dusting colour to create the background sky effect. Fill a small parchment piping bag with pale green royal icing (no tube is needed) and pipe two to three lines around the base of the cake. Fit a No. 1 writing tube to the bag and pipe grass on to the bottom quarter of the cake side, both above and on top of the base lines, to create a relief effect.

6 Add a small amount of royal icing to the side of the cake where the geese are to be positioned and place the off-set pieces on to the cake coating. Push very carefully to ensure each one is attached. Pipe a little more grass over the geese's feet.

Note

Any gold- or silver-coloured sections should always be removed before serving.

VARIATION *For this striking cake, separate run-outs have been built up to create an heraldic coat-of-arms (a club badge or insignia looks equally stunning). This was then positioned centrally beneath drapes rolled from Mexican Paste 2.*

*To finish, apply a little royal icing round the necks of the geese
and attach garlands of tiny Mexican Paste flowers.*

Ornate Quilling

While on holiday in Greece, I watched with interest as an old man worked with silver strips, bending and winding them into elaborate jewellery designs. This reminded me of the hours I spent as a child enjoying paper quilling. The two subjects, though employing different materials, are similar in technique.

For some years now I have been applying the technique of paper quilling to rolled fondant (sugarpaste), copying designs of wrought-iron work: arched gates with barley twist insets, fence panels with ornate scroll work and so on. There are many quilling shapes, but this design uses just the basic techniques.

R E Q U I R E M E N T S

- 20 cm (8") square cake coated with 900 g (2 lb) marzipan
- 900 g (2 lb) white rolled fondant (sugarpaste)
- greaseproof paper (baking parchment) and white card for templates
- Quick Release Sheet (QRS) or waxed paper
- work board
- Pure Mexican Paste
- edible food colours: green, brown, yellow and rust
- mint cutter or craft knife
- polythene (plastic) sheet
- modified quilling tool or cocktail sticks (toothpicks)
- sugar glue
- cake tilter
- scriber
- royal icing
- parchment piping bags (cones)
- No. 1.5 piping tube

QUILL SHAPES

Spiral, eyelet and teardrop: *Using a modified quilling tool or a pair of cocktail sticks, turn a strip on to its side, attach the tool to one end of the paste strip and turn in a clockwise motion to form a spiral. The spiral can then be cut at any time to produce an eyelet shape; apply a little sugar glue to the end to fasten. A teardrop shape is formed from an eyelet quill by pinching one side of the spiral.*

'S' shape: *Wind the paste from either end of a strip with a rotating action. First twist one end of the paste clockwise, then twist the opposite end of the paste clockwise forming an 'S' quill.*

'C' shape: *Wind the paste from either one or both ends of a strip, curling in towards the centre of the quill to form a 'C' shape.*

TEMPLATE

1 Cover the cake with the rolled fondant and allow to dry for approximately 24 hours. Cut a piece of greaseproof paper to fit the cake side, position over the quill pattern, redrawing to fit your cake if necessary (see Basic Techniques, pages 8–9) and trace. Position a piece of QRS or waxed paper over the design and place both on a work board.

Colour the Pure Mexican Paste as required – green, brown, yellow and rust have been used here. Working on one colour at a time, roll out thinly and cut narrow strips of paste with either a mint cutter or a craft knife. If using a mint cutter, cut each strip in half again lengthwise. Cover with a polythene sheet. Remove one strip at a time to work on; the size of the finished quill will depend on the length of the strip of paste, but do not cut the strip too long.

2 Make all the quill shapes in this way, then gently position on the master pattern over the scroll guide lines. Manoeuvre each quill into the correct area and adjust the shape as necessary. Continue with all the different colours and shapes as shown on the design until the master pattern is complete. Allow to dry for 24 hours.

3 Before applying the quills, place the cake on a tilter and gently scribe through the greaseproof paper pattern so that the main lines of your design are transferred on to the set fondant coating.

4 Using a little royal icing, attach the separate quills to the side of the cake in their appropriate positions, using the master pattern as your guide.

Complete the cake by piping the border using a No. 1.5 piping tube and yellow royal icing.

Template
Broderie Anglaise

Broderie anglaise is often associated with material where a pattern of holes is stitched around the edges to give a heavier look to the overall embroidery design. There are several ways of making broderie anglaise pieces for a cake, usually with cutters. I have adapted this style of side decoration to reflect the ornamental and colourful tops worn by the people of Greece on festive days. This template technique gives greater scope to the anglaise drop, allowing greater freedom of design.

REQUIREMENTS

- *20 cm (8") round cake coated with 800 g (1¾ lb) marzipan and covered with 900 g (2 lb) white rolled fondant (sugarpaste) and allowed to dry for 24 hours*
- *mint cutter*
- *sugar glue*
- *greaseproof paper (baking parchment) and cardboard for templates*
- *scissors*
- *Mexican Paste 2*
- *craft knife*
- *polythene (plastic) sheet*
- *eyelet cutters*
- *straight frill cutter*
- *edible food colours: lemon, violet, green*
- *dowel rods*
- *cake tilter*
- *royal icing*
- *parchment piping bags (cones)*
- *No. 0 and 2 piping tubes*

1 Cover the cake with the white rolled fondant and allow to dry for 24 hours. Using the cake trimmings, roll a strip of rolled fondant to fit the cake circumference and trim to 0.5 cm (¼") in depth using a mint cutter. Paint a band of sugar glue approximately 0.5 cm (¼") down from the top of the cake and attach the fixing strip. Leave to one side to skin over.

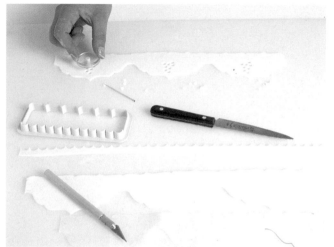

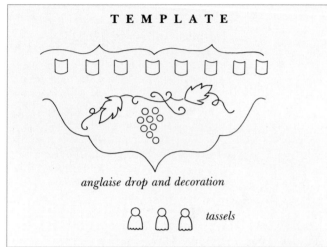

TEMPLATE

anglaise drop and decoration

tassels

2 To prepare the template, measure the circumference of the fixing strip and cut a greaseproof paper strip to fit. Fold the strip into six equal sections and trace the design given on to one of the sections. Transfer on to a piece of white cardboard and cut out carefully with scissors.

Roll out a sheet of white Mexican Paste 2 and cut round the cardboard template with a craft knife. Repeat to give two patterned strips. Place one under a polythene sheet to prevent skinning. With eyelet cutters remove groups of small holes to resemble bunches of grapes.

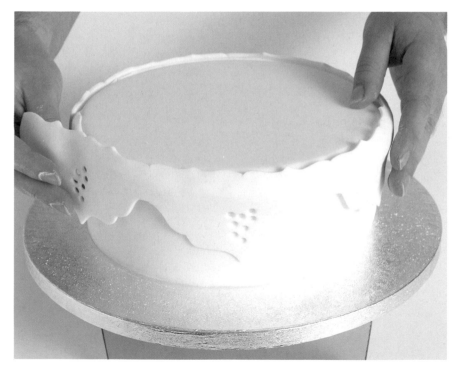

3 Paint the fixing strip with sugar glue and gently apply the first anglaise section, taking care not to stretch or distort it. Repeat for the second section, ensuring the joins line up and butt closely together. Ease the upper portion of the anglaise sections to follow the curve of the cake.

4 Roll a sheet of Mexican Paste 2 and cut out a shallow band with the straight frill cutter. Trim to approximately 1.25 cm (½″) in depth with the plain side of the cutter. Paint the base of the cake with sugar glue and attach the band, butting the joins carefully. Allow the whole cake to dry for approximately 24 hours.

To make the paste ribbons, use green Mexican Paste and follow the instructions for the Ribbon Insertion cake (see pages 42–45). Attach the ribbon pieces round the top edge of the anglaise drops with royal icing.

5 Pipe around the cut-out grapes in deep violet-coloured royal icing using a No. 0 tube. The tube should be the same distance from the surface of the eyelet as the diameter of the tube tip. Pipe freehand vines and leaves with a No. 0 tube and green royal icing.

6 Over-pipe all the edges of paste anglaise and frill sections with a fine rope border in deep lemon using a No. 0 tube. Pipe groups of tiny freehand dots in lemon, green and violet to enhance the area between the anglaise drops and the lower frill band. Pipe a fine herringbone shell border using a No. 2 writing tube and white royal icing. Enhance with tiny dots of violet and green royal icing.

For the finishing touch, pipe a selection of deep-lemon-coloured tassels on to waxed paper with a No. 0 writing tube. Pipe the upright strings first then pipe a bulb directly at the upper edge. Pipe a few lines across the join. Allow to set for 2 to 3 hours in a warm dry place. Attach the off-set tassels to the edges of the anglaise drops with a little royal icing.

Simple Bas-Relief

Originally from the world of art, bas-relief has been adapted to sugarcraft to give texture, extra dimension and interest to cake surfaces. It is most commonly found adorning the top of a cake. However, I have developed this technique further to give a better concept of its uses when applied to the cake side.

Bas-relief is found in several forms and there are many different techniques that can be used. For the purposes of this design I have chosen a quick, simple and basic form of bas-relief, where the relief pieces are made as built-up, off-set items, which are then attached to the cake side.

REQUIREMENTS

- 20 cm (8") square cake coated with 900 g (2 lb) marzipan, covered with 900 g (2 lb) rolled fondant (sugarpaste), coloured jade, and allowed to dry for approximately 24 hours
- plain white paper
- Mexican Paste 2
- polythene (plastic) sheet
- Quick Release Sheet (QRS) or waxed paper
- adhesive tape
- edible food colours: various
- cutters
- sugar glue
- craft knife
- paintbrushes
- fine dried herb stems
- tweezers
- small ball mould
- royal icing
- parchment piping bags (cones)
- edible dusting colours: various
- cocktail stick (toothpick)
- modelling tools
- tiny plunger blossom cutter
- cake tilter
- clear alcohol, such as vodka
- feeler gauge or cranked palette knife (spatula)
- clay gun (optional)

Swiss   Red Indian   English

Japanese   Dutch   African

JAPANESE GIRL

All the figures are modelled using the same basic techniques. Here is just one example to highlight how the figures are built-up.

Place the main outline drawing under a piece of QRS or waxed paper, and secure with a little adhesive tape. Roll and cut a strip of paste and position within the main outline to make a base to build on. With pale flesh-coloured Mexican Paste 2, mould and model 6 separate pieces of paste as follows: two of the same size – one to create a flattened peardrop for the body, the other shaped into a rounded head using the small ball mould; two smaller pieces of paste rolled into sausage shapes for legs; two tiny balls for hands.

Glue the body to the base strip, then position the head piece so it overlaps the tip of the pear-shaped body. Mark the eyes with a miniature modelling tool and use the edge of a medium blossom cutter for the mouth. Shape two small oval balls of white paste for the feet, then roll and cut two tiny sections of black paste and attach to one side of the feet to form the soles of the shoes. Attach two fine 'V' shapes of black paste to the top of the feet with sugar glue to complete the shoes. Attach the feet to one end of each leg, and attach the legs to the body, covering the base strip.

Roll out a piece of coloured paste for the kimono and cut a V-shaped neckline. Coat the body and legs with sugar glue (avoiding the neck area), and cover with the kimono piece. Gently smooth over to secure the paste to the body and legs. Cut around the outline of the bas-relief character and remove excess paste. Cut a strip of contrasting coloured paste for the cummerbund and attach to the waist area with sugar glue.

To form the arms, roll two small finger shapes of flesh-coloured paste. To make the sleeves, roll out a piece of Mexican Paste 2 in the kimono colour. Cut into a square, then cut across the diagonal to form two triangles. Paint a line of sugar glue from apex point of each triangle down to centre of the base. Position arm along the centre line. Coat one side of the triangular shape with sugar glue and fold in half to form sleeve. Glue and attach to the side of the bodice below the neck by gently pushing the upper arm portion into place. Bend the arms to shape at this stage and glue the tiny hands into position at the ends of the sleeves.

To make the hair, roll a medium-sized finger of black paste and pull down in the centre to form a slight point. Coat the top and sides of the head with sugar glue and place hair in position. Roll a ball of black paste and attach to the top of the head for the bun. Cut two fine stems of any dried herb and push into two tiny balls of paste. Insert into hair with tweezers to form ornamental combs. Add two flowers to the hair, made using tiny plunger blossom cutters. Fine detail may be added with royal icing, dusting powder or painted with food colour at this point.

71

1 Begin by copying each of the motifs and transferring the main outlines on to a sheet of plain white paper. Ensure that the picture faces the same way as the original. There should be two identical pictures for each of the characters, one the master, the other a main outline drawing. Use Mexican Paste 2 for all the modelling work, and colour as appropriate. Different 'nationalities' can be created by altering the colours used for the flesh tones, changing the colour and style of hair, and dressing each 'child' in its own national costume. As you complete each figure, cover with a sheet of polythene so that the paste remains malleable until all twelve characters are ready to be mounted on the cake.

2 To prepare the background detail on the cake side, mix some brilliant silver dusting powder with a little clear alcohol and paint cloud shapes as shown (brilliant white food colour may be used as an alternative).

3 To create the grass effect, dab a wide flat brush into green paste food colour and lightly wipe upwards over the lower edge of the cake. Partially knead some black food colour with some white Mexican Paste 2 until it becomes grey and mottled. Paint approximately 1 cm (½″) of the cakeboard and the bottom of the cake below the grass markings with sugar glue. Roll small balls of grey paste and squash on to the cake side and the cakeboard over the glued area to form a cobble-stone footpath.

4 Remove each character from the waxed paper by gently sliding a cranked palette knife or feeler gauge underneath. Attach each bas-relief child to the cake side using a little royal icing so that the feet just rest on the footpath.

5 With dark jade-coloured paste, cut fine strips to represent the ribbon of unity. Twist and attach to the children's hands with a little royal icing. Join tiny plunger blossom flowers to the ribbon at random intervals.

The theme of this delicately tinted cake is one of international friendship and peace.

Extension Work and Lace

Extension work is a name given to fine lines piped on to bridge lines. The bridge lines support the extension lines, holding them away from the surface of the cake side. Extension lines are usually piped vertically all round the sides, but different patterns may be formed by piping the lines at angles, slanting left and right. For a gravity-defying effect, the cake may also be turned upside down, the bridge and extension work piped and allowed to set, and the cake returned right way up again.

Lace pieces are often used to enhance extension work. These off-set sections, piped in royal icing, usually resemble lace, hence the name. When piping these delicate pieces, it is important that the tiny lines touch each other and all joins are sound, otherwise it will be impossible to remove them intact from the waxed paper. If piping lace for the first time it is best to use a piping tube that you are already confident with handling; once you have learned and perfected the basic technique, progress to a finer tube.

REQUIREMENTS

- *20 cm (8″) square cake coated with 900 g (2 lb) marzipan, covered with 900 g (2 lb) grey rolled fondant (sugarpaste) and allowed to dry for 24 hours*
- *waxed paper or Quick Release Sheet*
- *greaseproof paper (baking parchment) templates*
- *parchment piping bags (cones)*
- *royal icing*
- *No. 00, 0, 1 and 2 piping tubes*
- *curved former*
- *paintbrushes*
- *edible dusting colours: pale pink, pale blue*
- *glass-headed dressmakers' pins*
- *scriber*
- *edible food colours: black, pale pink*
- *cake tilter*

TEMPLATE

1 The lace should be piped before beginning work on the cake itself, using waxed paper or Quick Release Sheet (QRS). Position the lace design template beneath the waxed paper and fill a small parchment piping bag with royal icing and attach a No. 00, 0 or 1 writing tube. Pipe a few pieces of lace and place these into the curved former before they start to skin over. Continue until there are enough lace pieces for the cake, remembering to pipe out more lace than required to allow for breakages. Leave to set in a dry, warm place for approximately 12 hours. When completely set, use a soft, dry brush and dusting powder to apply colour.

2 To prepare the cake, measure and make a template to fit the cake side and trace the design for the extension work and bridgework as given for this cake. With glass-headed dressmakers' pins, hold the template against the side of the cake and scribe the top guide line for the extension work through on to the cake surface. Simply mark the tops of the loops for the bridgework with the pointed tip of the scriber.

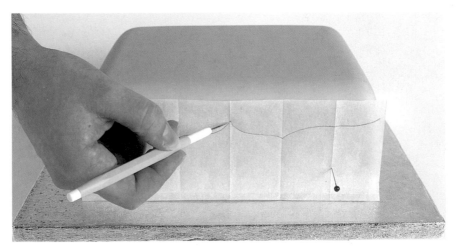

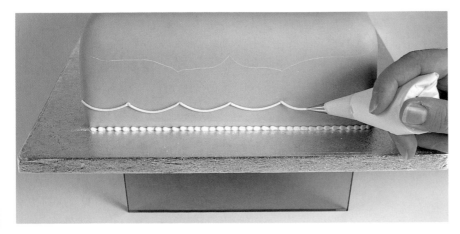

3 Position the cake on a tilter; it is particularly important to use a tilter when piping bridge and extension work. With a No. 1 writing tube pipe a fine snail's-trail border at the base of the cake. To create the bridgework, fill a small parchment piping bag with royal icing and attach a No. 2 tube. Pipe a series of loops round the cake, using the marks made with the point of the scriber as a guide. Continuing with a No. 1 tube, over-pipe these loops 5 more times so that 6 lines are built out from the side of the cake. Leave to dry for an hour.

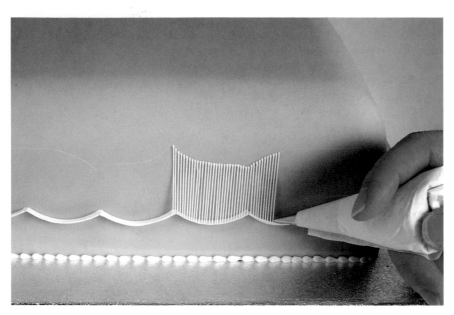

4 To form the extension lines, fill a small parchment piping bag with royal icing and attach a fine tube (No. 00, 0 or 1 depending on your competence). Pipe a vertical line from the top of the scribed pattern down to the bridgework. Keep the lines pulled taut and parallel at all times. The distance between each line should be the same as the thickness of the piping tube.

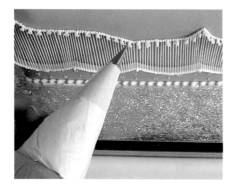

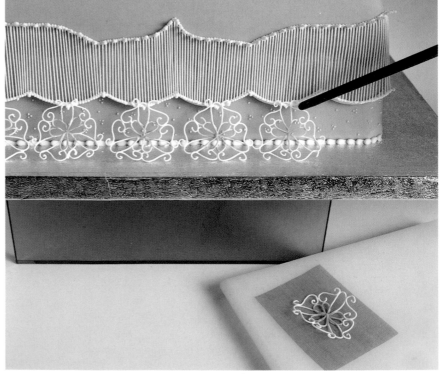

5 Pipe tiny groups of dot embroidery beneath the bridgework. Then, pipe a diamond-shaped picot edge along the top of the extension lines using a No. 0 piping tube (see Basic Techniques, page 10).

6 Finally, apply the curved off-set lace pieces to the base of the cake and attach the top edges to the bridgework with a little royal icing.

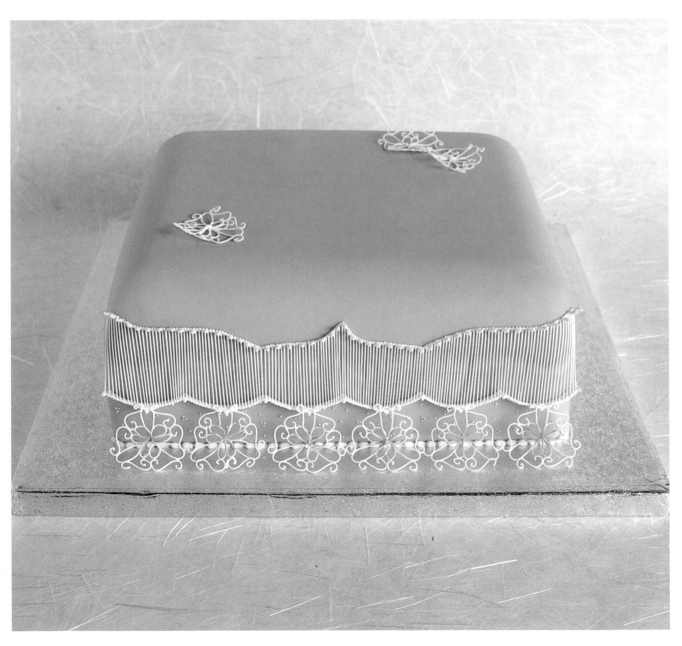

*This style of cake decorating is very fine and suits most wedding and celebration cakes.
However, you must allow yourself plenty of time to complete the work as it cannot
be rushed. All cakes decorated in this way, though fragile, travel well, providing they
are properly boxed and have a foam sheet underneath to act as a shock absorber.*

Criqué Work

Criqué work is a technique I have developed and perfected over many years. It works best when carried out on a straight-sided cake, such as an extended octagonal, hexagonal, diamond or square cake.

However, with skill and practice, the technique can also be applied to curved cakes. The literal translation of 'criqué' is inlet or cove. The secret of flawless criqué work is in the preparation of the cake base.

REQUIREMENTS

- *20 cm (8″) hexagonal cake*
- *900 g (2 lb) marzipan*
- *900 g (2 lb) rolled fondant (sugarpaste)*
- *cardboard for template*
- *sharp knife*
- *melon baller or parisienne cutter*
- *paintbrushes*
- *apricot masking*
- *edible food colours: cream, brown, violet-blue*
- *clear alcohol, such as vodka*
- *Mexican Paste 2*
- *craft knife*
- *royal icing*
- *parchment piping bags (cones)*
- *cake tilter*
- *No. 2, 42 and 44 piping tubes*
- *miniature violet arrangements in vases, made from Mexican Paste*

TEMPLATE

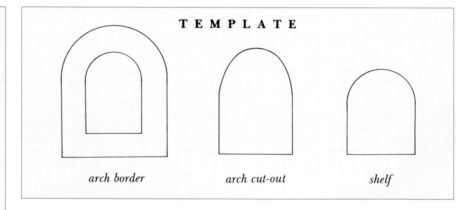

arch border　　　*arch cut-out*　　　*shelf*

1 First make a cardboard template to form the criqué area. I have used an arch shape. Position the template centrally against the cake side before applying the marzipan. Use a sharp pointed knife to cut into the cake round the criqué template about 2.5–3 cm (1–1½″). Remove the template.

2 Using a curved-bladed tool (either a melon baller or a parisienne cutter), scoop out the cake mixture from the top of the criqué area to the cut base line. The walls of the criqué section should be slightly curved from top to bottom. Remove enough cake so the criqué section will remain distinct after the marzipan and rolled fondant have been applied.

3 Turn the cake on its side and paint the criqué section with apricot masking. Marzipan the criqué first, then cover the cake with marzipan in the usual way.

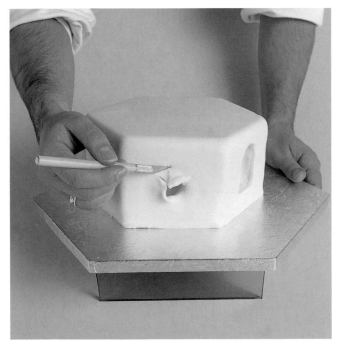

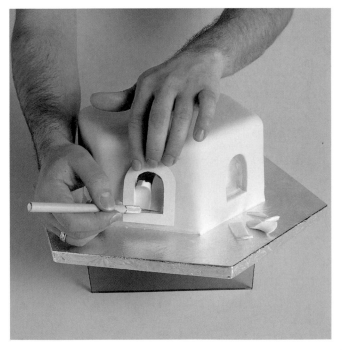

4 Either freehand or using the criqué border template as a guide, cut through to the criqué; remove the marzipan to expose the criqué area beneath. Smooth the edges of the marzipan with your fingers.

5 Cover the cake with honey-brown rolled fondant. Using the criqué border template as a guide, cut away the excess paste to expose the criqué areas as before. Allow to dry for 24 hours.

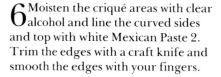

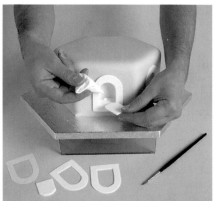

7 Cut a second cardboard template for the arch. Roll out a piece of white Mexican Paste 2 then cut out an arch border to fit round the criqué area. Allow to skin for about one hour until firm enough to handle. Attach the arch to the cake side using a little royal icing. Cut a shelf from the Mexican Paste and model to fit the base of the criqué, as shown; it should protrude slightly to form a ledge. Allow to skin for approximately one hour. Attach to the base of the criqué with royal icing.

6 Moisten the criqué areas with clear alcohol and line the curved sides and top with white Mexican Paste 2. Trim the edges with a craft knife and smooth the edges with your fingers.

8 Divide each cake side into two by eye, making a mark at the top of the cake with a small dot of royal icing. Using white royal icing and a No. 42 fine toothed tube, pipe two shallow dropped loops above the criqué area. Fill a medium parchment piping bag with white royal icing and drag a No. 44 tube twice down each corner of the hexagonal cake to produce the uprights of the Grecian columns.

9 Pipe a line along the bottom of the cake with a No. 42 tube to form the border. Pipe a No. 44 line to the bottom of the columns and over-pipe with a No. 42 line to form the bases. Pipe the scrolls at the tops of the columns with a No. 2 writing tube, using a series of piped circles. Repeat on all sides.

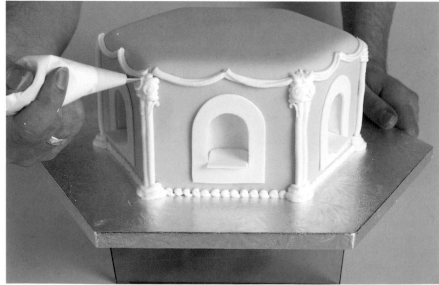

*To complete the cake, position and attach
a miniature vase of violets on each shelf as shown.*

Renaissance Embroidery Cake

Embroidery has been used to embellish materials of all descriptions for hundreds of years, transforming humble items into intricate works of art.

Cake sides can be adorned in the same way using direct piping both with and without piping tubes. Inspiration for designs can be found in modern-day embroidery transfer patterns, a rich source of ideas for both novice and experienced confectioners alike. A piece of material or small sections from a bride's dress can be copied on to the side of a wedding cake, thereby linking a design from the gown to a tiered centrepiece. Using a coloured rolled fondant (sugarpaste) base with the same-coloured piping produces a delicate, textured and eye-catching finish to any cake. However, I have chosen to use dark and vibrant colours piped on an ivory-coloured 20 cm (8″) square base for a strong contrast on this striking Renaissance embroidery cake.

REQUIREMENTS

- 20 cm (8″) square cake coated with 900 g (2 lb) marzipan and allowed to dry for 24 hours
- 900 g (2 lb) ivory-coloured rolled fondant (sugarpaste)
- greaseproof paper (baking parchment) template
- glass-headed dressmakers' pins
- scriber
- edible food colours: pale and dark green, turquoise and royal blue, lemon and cream
- royal icing
- parchment piping bags (cones)
- No. 0, 1 and 3 piping tubes
- cake tilter
- edible gold dust or lustre powder
- clear alcohol, such as vodka

TEMPLATE

Notes

The scribed pattern on the cake side has been highlighted with a marker pen for photographic purposes only.

Remove all items coated with gold colour before cutting and serving the cake.

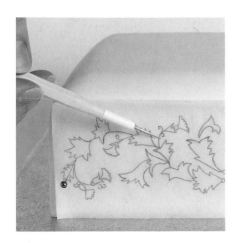

1 Cover the cake with ivory-coloured rolled fondant and allow to dry for 2–3 days. Cut a greaseproof paper template to fit the cake side. Copy the design on to the paper template. Place the template against the cake side, ensuring that the graphite lines are facing outwards, and pin into position with glass-headed dressmakers' pins. Transcribe the design on to the firm fondant by scratching through the template with a scriber. Remove the template.

2 For the flowerheads, place lemon-coloured royal icing that has been toned down with a little cream food colour into a small parchment piping bag fitted with a No. 0 piping tube. Hold the piping bag at a slight angle with the tube tip the same distance from the cake as the diameter of the hole. Pressure the icing on to the fondant and drag the tip of the piping tube along the scribed lines. If the bag and tube are held correctly the pattern will not be affected by gravity and the design will build up exactly where required.

3 For the foliage and detail, fill four small parchment piping bags with royal icing coloured as follows: pale green; dark green; pale turquoise blue; and darker royal blue. These bags do not need tubes but should have a fine hole cut in the tips. Outline each section of the scribed pattern in the appropriate colour as a guide.

4 Cut the tips off the piping bags containing the pale green and pale turquoise blue royal icings at a slight angle to give more defined and larger holes. Drag the tip of the bag containing the turquoise royal icing over the fondant surface using long, continuous strokes, filling in the sections of foliage outlined in this colour. Repeat this technique using the pale green royal icing until all the foliage has been completed.

5 Continue by over-piping the pale blue with the darker royal blue icing and the pale green with the darker green icing as shown. This will add depth to your design. Pipe the dots with a parchment piping bag containing the darker green icing and a No. 0 tube. Hold the tip of the tube at a right angle to the cake coating, with the distance between the tube tip and the fondant equal to the diameter of the tube. Apply pressure to the bag until a small dot of the required size is formed, then release the pressure keeping the tip of the tube in contact with the surface of the royal icing. Lift the tube with a slight rotation of the hand to ensure there is no take-off point evident.

6 Mix a little gold powder or gold lustre with alcohol and paint on to the darker green areas to enhance the overall design.

VARIATION *The same design has been adapted and extended to cover the sides and top of this smaller cake.*

*Finally, pipe a plain white shell border with a No. 3 piping tube and
add small dark green in-fill dots piped with a No. 1 piping tube.*

USEFUL SUPPLIERS
AND ADDRESSES

THE BRITISH SUGARCRAFT GUILD Wellington House, Messeter Place, Eltham, London SE9 5DP.

CAKE ART LTD Wholesale suppliers of icings and equipment. Unit 16, Crown Close, Crown Industrial Estate, Priors Wood, Taunton, Somerset TA2 8RX.

SUGARCRAFT SUPPLIERS PME (HARROW) LTD Suppliers of decorating equipment. Brember Road, South Harrow, Middlesex HA2 8UN.

JF RENSHAW LTD Suppliers of icings. Locks Lane, Mitcham, Surrey CR4 2XG.

ESSEX ICING CENTRE Suppliers of materials and equipment. 20 Western Road, Billericay, Essex CM12 9DZ.

INVICTA BAKEWARE LTD Manufacturers and suppliers of bakery equipment. Westgate Business Park, Westgate Carr Road, Pickering, North Yorkshire YO18 8LX.

CRANHAM CATERING Suppliers of materials and equipment. 95 Front Lane, Cranham, Upminster, Essex RM14 1XN.

CRAIGMILLAR Suppliers of icings and cake mixes. Stadium Road, Bromborough, Wirral, Merseyside LO2 3NU.

PROMODEM LTD Technical consultancy and suppliers of QRS and cake tilters. 141 Grange Road, Great Burstead, Billericay, Essex CM11 2SA.

SQUIRES KITCHEN Squire House, 3 Waverley Lane, Farnham, Surrey GU9 8BB.

E RUSSUM & SONS Edward House, Tenter Street, Rotherham.

THE HOUSE OF SUGARCRAFT Suppliers of flower cutters, powder and paste colours and piping tubes. Unit 10, Broxhead Industrial Estate, Lindford Road, Bordon, Hampshire GU35 0NY.

CEL CAKES Suppliers of modelling tools, containers and display cabinets. Springfield House, Gate Helmsley, York, North Yorkshire YO4 1NF.

JENNY CAMPBELL TRADING/B R MATTHEWS AND SON 12 Gypsy Hill, Upper Norwood, London SE19 1NN.

CYNTHIA VENN 3 Anker Lane, Stubbington, Fareham, Hampshire PO14 3HF.

KNIGHTSBRIDGE BUSINESS CENTRE (WILTON UK) Knightsbridge, Cheltenham, Gloucestershire GL51 9TA.

RAINBOW RIBBONS Unit D5, Romford Seedbed Centre, Davidson Way, Romford, Essex RM7 0AZ.

ADRIAN WESTROPE Courses and demonstrations offered internationally on all aspects of sugarcraft. Enquiries c/o Promodem Ltd, 141 Grange Road, Great Burstead, Billericay, Essex CM11 2SA.

NORTH AMERICA

ICES (INTERNATIONAL CAKE EXPLORATION SOCIETY) membership enquiries: 3087–30th St. S.W., Ste.101, Grandville, MI 49418.

MAID OF SCANDINAVIA Equipment, supplies, courses, magazine *Mailbox News*. 3244 Raleigh Avenue, Minneapolis, MN 55416.

WILTON ENTERPRISES INC 2240 West 75th Street, Woodridge, Illinois 60517.

HOME CAKE ARTISTRY INC 1002 North Central, Suite 511, Richardson, Texas 75080.

LORRAINE'S INC 148 Broadway, Hanover, MA 02339.

CREATIVE TOOLS LTD 3 Tannery Court, Richmond Hill, Ontario, Canada L4C 7V5.

MCCALL'S SCHOOL OF CAKE DECORATING INC 3810 Bloor Street, Islington, Ontario, Canada M9B 6C2.

AUSTRALIA

AUSTRALIAN NATIONAL CAKE DECORATORS' ASSOCIATION PO Box 321, Plympton, SA 5038.

CAKE DECORATING ASSOCIATION OF VICTORIA President, Shirley Vaas, 4 Northcote Road, Ocean Grove, Victoria 3226.

CAKE DECORATING GUILD OF NEW SOUTH WALES President, Fay Gardiner, 4 Horsley Cres, Melba, Act, 2615.

CAKE DECORATING ASSOCIATION OF TASMANIA Secretary, Jenny Davis, 29 Honolulu Street, Midway Point, Tasmania 7171.

CAKE DECORATORS' ASSOCIATION OF SOUTH AUSTRALIA Secretary, Lorraine Joliffe, Pindari, 12 Sussex Crescent, Morphet Vale, SA 5162.

FER LEWIS, CAKE ORNAMENT COMPANY 156 Alfred Street, Fortitude Valley, Brisbane 4006.

NEW ZEALAND

NEW ZEALAND CAKE DECORATORS' GUILD Secretary, Julie Tibble, 78 Kirk Street, Otaki, Wellington.

DECOR CAKES RSA Arcade, 435 Great South Road, Otahaha.

SOUTH AFRICA

SOUTH AFRICAN SUGARCRAFT GUILD National Office, 1 Tuzla Mews, 187 Smit Street, Fairlan 2195.

JEM CUTTERS PO Box 115, Kloof, 3 Nisbett Road, Pinetown 3600, South Africa.

INDEX

ACKNOWLEDGEMENTS

I would like to thank so many people who have helped me, from providing endless cups of coffee to suffering numb finger tips from the countless pages of typing. I wish to thank my parents for being there at all times and my brother Neil for his continued support; my partner in 'crime' Linda, without whose fingers these pages would never have been written; my great friend Marie Herbstritt who provided the mini violets for the criqué cake (page 80); my past and present students as well as the countless friends in the many guilds I have had the pleasure of demonstrating to; David and Malcolm at PME for their support; my friends Pat and Angela, Carole and Trevor; Dan Tabor, my first true ICES friend; and all at Letts for their time and patience; thanks too to Promodem Ltd for the extensive use of their cake tilter.